SOCIAL PLANNING AND SOCIAL CHANGE

PRENTICE-HALL, INC., Englewood Cliffs, New Jersey

Social Science Foundations of Social Welfare Series

Robert Morris and Wyatt Jones, editors

SOCIAL PLANNING AND SOCIAL CHANGE

ROBERT R. MAYER

University of North Carolina at Chapel Hill

P-13-817270-6   C-13-817288-9

Library of Congress Catalog Card Number: 75-151511
Printed in the United States of America

Current printing (last number):
10   9   8   7   6   5   4   3   2   1

PRENTICE-HALL INTERNATIONAL, INC., London
PRENTICE-HALL OF AUSTRALIA, PTY. INC., Sydney
PRENTICE-HALL OF CANADA, LTD., Toronto
PRENTICE-HALL OF INDIA PRIVATE LIMITED, New Delhi
PRENTICE-HALL OF JAPAN, INC., Tokyo

to PETER, KEVIN, and TONY

FOREWORD

Robert Mayer presents us with a new diagnostic tool for achieving social goals; the analysis of the social system in which individual (pathological, problematic) behavior is contained. He contrasts social system manipulation with direct service approaches. His argument is that attempts to achieve social values might proceed more effectively by analysis and change of the environmental or social system constraints and determinants of a particular problem area rather than by direct interpersonal work with target populations.

Professor Mayer suggests that there are three major modes for changing the social system: (1) changing the *combination* of persons who participate in the system; (2) changing the *roles* people play in that system; (3) changing the *statuses* of the persons in that system.

I agree with him that this type of analysis is enormously important, underdeveloped, and potentially powerful: It is intellectually linked to the revolution of curricular perspectives in schools of social work occurring over the last decade or so. In this revolution the society, not the individual, is seen as the locus of pathology; and sociological concepts and analysis replace or intrude upon psychoanalytic and social psychological perspectives.

There are, however, some limits and problems in the use of this approach that I would like to mention. I do not see the problems I am going to mention as insurmountable or as necessarily contradictory to Professor Mayer's analysis. Indeed at some points he notes them in his presentation. Rather these limitations are complicating factors which lead us to proceed with caution.

My feeling is that Professor Mayer's approach will remain incomplete until (1) it articulates the boundary of the social system approach with direct provision of services; (2) it articulates the boundaries of the social system approach with, for want of a better word, macro-societal approaches; and (3) it develops a "cost-benefit" analysis of the potential of each option for particular problems. Let me discuss each point in turn.

SOCIAL STRUCTURE AND DIRECT SERVICES

As sociological and economic perspectives have been applied to the welfare scene it has become fashionable to play down the provision of direct services—either they are seen as ineffective paternalism or as merely ineffective. Economists, such as Milton Friedman, deeply committed to the links between individual liberty and market capitalism, argue that wherever possible a service should be provided only if the individual wants and is willing to pay for it. Friedman would make enough money available for the poor to have some choice. But even less individualistically-oriented scholars have damned the direct provision of service as ineffective.

I would make two points: First, as long as tax dollars are used for a program some governmental regulation will ensue. For instance, assume that we did not provide direct services to the blind, or rehabilitation workshops for the physically handicapped. Instead we allow the clients of these organizations to use governmentally provided money for their own ends. I suspect we would soon find ourselves *either* controlling and sanctioning clients who misused these funds *or* sanctioning and controlling organizations that were major purveyors of goods and services to these clients. (I should point out that as far as I can tell most of Friedman's analysis ignores problems of externalities of behavior and the problem of public goods.)

Second, and more relevant to Professor Mayer's argument, we need to know when direct services are effective and when not. In drawing on Jacob's description of teeming streets, Mayer contrasts control of crime through typical delinquency projects and control of crime through land use planning, the basic idea being that if streets are busy and crowded crime goes down. But it is obvious that the major way you control crime (directly) is through building up your police force and surveillance apparatus; that is real direct service! (It may be that in the long run crime can only be controlled *indirectly* through massive moral reintegration of society, and the sense of shared community. But moral reintegration is such a long range and diffuse goal that it is probably beyond the purview of reasonable social policy.)

Many direct social service programs (broadly defined) are very effective, at least as measured by customer satisfaction. This may be a definitional problem, but as I view the social service arena I see lots of organizations like Boy's Clubs in urban slums, Boy Scouts in the suburbs, and YMCA's all over that are teeming with clients. I see county agents developing the skills of farmers and I see public health nurses doing a terrific job of direct service.

One general proposition might be that *the more the target population has values, cognitive and physical skills, or subgroup norms that inhibit the utilization of, or response to, direct services, the more structural rearrangement is likely to be called for.* For example, senior citizens often have problems of physical mobility as well as motivational problems that impede utilization of senior citizen centers. Some senior citizen centers have done a good job of overcoming this problem: they have a volunteer jitney service.

SOCIAL SYSTEM AND SOCIETY

Professor Mayer uses a weak definition of social system, essentially any bounded pattern of interaction. But a key question is how strong is the pattern and how bounded? Phrased differently, how autonomous is the focal social system and its major components. Are the major elements of the system heavily dependent upon or intertwined with the larger society or are they only peripherally attached? (Incidentally, Mayer's discussion of cases shows he is aware of both the interdependence of the systems he is analyzing and their complexity.)

Some of Mayer's cases can be used to illustrate my point. He reviews the problem of social integration of the aged. We have a diverse set of public policies and market mechanisms for housing people in need or people with different tastes. If they have enough money some senior citizens solve their sociability problems by moving to St. Petersburg or, at a later stage, by moving into senior citizen villages. For those without money, a variety of public facilities are available with a range of policies governing their usage. I take the allocation of the aged among public units to be a relatively *autonomous* policy. It has few effects outside the housing project and its administration. And Mayer's prescriptions for creating housing communities for the aged in such a way as to increase social integration seem quite reasonable.

But some of his cases are related to highly intertwined and dependent processes. For instance, he links crime rates to land use patterns. Land use patterns are a dependent function of basic values. Survey after survey has shown that most Americans, for most of their lives, prefer to own a detached home on a large lot. Except for a few kooks and/or professors and a few ethnic minorities with strong familial and communal ties, most Americans don't want to live in Jane Jacob's romanticized urban villages; thus unless building, land, and transportation costs thrust us into urban villages, it will be hard to effect crime rates by changing land use patterns.

Another instance of an interdependent process and status is treated in his review of Carpenter's study of able bodied men on skid row. This study shows that men on skid row change their behavior for the better after they reach 65. Age of legitimate retirement (withdrawal) from the labor force is highly dependent upon the broader society. It will be just very hard to effect the social definitions of legitimate age of withdrawal in the society. And individual definition of "success" and "failure" in relation to such withdrawal cannot be easily manipulated. A man's whole self-concept is involved. There may be some ways to redefine these status-related social-psychological criteria for sub-groups in the population, but it will not be easy.

I would suggest that, everything else being equal, *the more autonomous the social system condition that is desired to be changed, and the less value attached to the condition or pattern by the target population, the easier it will be to manipulate.*

COST-BENEFIT ANALYSIS OF POLICY OPTIONS

There is a hidden wisdom in direct service approaches. Even when they have high economic costs, they may have few social and political costs. It may "be expensive" to retrain 5,000 workers that actually retain jobs in their new occupations. It may be very easy to lower unemployment rates and get 500,000 people back to work by manipulating the economy. On a narrow view of the problem, obviously you manipulate the economy. But social problems are not to be treated in isolation and if manipulating the economy to lower unemployment leads to high rates of inflation, indirect social, economic, and political costs may be very high. By and large, direct service solutions are specific and focused, so they rarely raise widespread political problems. (Of course, when people are clamoring for a solution to a problem, such as crime, and will not really consider a raise in taxes, one can ask whether the clamor is real, manipulated, widespread, or a red herring for something else.)

Analysis of political and social cost must look to the *spillover* costs and benefits of solutions proposed. Costs and benefits of spillover must be calculated for *ends* and *means*. Few social scientists would turn back the clock on school integration. Yet, no one, least of all the U. S. Supreme Court foresaw the enormous costs and consequences of desegregating the schools. My general point is that for Mayer's social system approach to be truly efficacious it must depend upon not only a finely tuned and specific diagnosis but a deep analysis of political, economic, and social costs and benefits. The kind of planning Mayer calls for cannot be done in a vacuum.

It may be that social system cost-benefit analysis would lead us to be more cautious than we have been in advocating structural change. And Mayer is aware of this dilemma. Yet his basic strategy is, I think, sound. Change will occur with or without the social scientist or planner. The job of the social planner is to use the best information and sharpest concepts at his disposal (hopefully avoiding current faddish rhetoric). With further development of the kinds of tools Professor Mayer suggests, we may move farther along the road to effective social policy.

Mayer N. Zald
Vanderbilt University

PREFACE

The present volume grew out of two very fruitful years of study at the Florence Heller Graduate School for Advanced Studies in Social Welfare, at Brandeis University. This association provided an opportunity to find some answers to intellectual problems which have confronted those engaged in social planning. What constitutes the special subject matter of social planning? What is the peculiar competence of the social planner?

The answers which I found are embodied in a planning model called *social-structural change*. The purpose of this book is to describe this model and to demonstrate its conceptual utility by analyzing cases in which it applies.

In Chapter 1, I attempt to outline the intellectual problem by assessing the present state of thinking about social planning. Chapter 2 consists of an elaboration of the nature of social-structural change. It gleans, from sociological theory, reasonable and discriminating definitions of social structure and social change. Chapters 3, 4, and 5 represent an analysis of cases that conform to these definitions. The analysis is guided by two questions which are fundamental to constructing a planning model: (1) how are problems translated into social-structural terms, and (2) what tools of intervention are available to accomplish social-structural change?

In Chapter 6, the results of this analysis are recapitulated in the form of a planning model. This recapitulation involves filling in some logical pieces missing from the analysis because of the selective nature of the cases involved.

The book concludes with a discussion, in Chapter 7, of the implications of this new conceptual model for practice and education in the socially-oriented professions.

The author is deeply indebted to the Florence Heller Graduate School, its faculty and students whose stimulation and encouragement are reflected in these pages. Special appreciation is extended to Professors Robert Morris, Robert Perlman, and Roland Warren of Brandeis University and James Davis of Dartmouth College whose ideas inspired this volume and whose guidance was keen and unfailing.

I would also like to recognize a long-standing indebtedness to Ernest Greenwood of the University of California whose teachings in the philosophy of science undergird this effort.

The editorial suggestions of Wyatt C. Jones greatly enhanced the manuscript.

Last but not least, I would like to express appreciation to my students in city planning at the University of North Carolina whose provocative questions improved the treatment of this subject.

My work on this book was made possible by a Special Research Fellowship (1F3 MH-36, 052-01 BEH-A) from the National Institute of Mental Health.

CONTENTS

FIGURES

Chapter 1

A NEW PERSPECTIVE
FOR SOCIAL PLANNING

INTRODUCTION

The subject of this book, social planning and social change, stems from two different but interrelated interests. One is the effort by the socially-oriented professions to derive from the social sciences a foundation for practice. The other is a growing conviction reflected in public debate that current approaches to solving social problems are inadequate.

The social sciences have been a subject of growing interest among the socially-oriented professions as attempts are made to build a scientific foundation for problem-solving. This interest has been characteristic not only of social work but of education, public health, medicine, and city planning. This book adds to such foundation-building by drawing upon knowledge from one of the social sciences—sociology.

Previous efforts to relate science to practice have often been characterized by an encyclopedic approach. They have accepted existing models of practice and surveyed the social sciences for knowledge which would be relevant or informative for that model. Such efforts result in a kind of catalog of concepts or schools of thought which are placed at the disposal of the practitioner to apply as best he can.

My approach differs from this tradition. It is in the more recent trend of model building. It starts with theory and derives a new model of practice. Relying on social systems theory the model constitutes a new diagnostic tool for achieving social goals. As such it represents a new model of practice in social planning.

This interest in social science as a basis for practice has been accelerated by current events. A new mood is reflected in current public expressions of concern with today's social problems.[1] Public debate is increasingly premised on the assumption that something is wrong with either the way things are organized or with the socially prescribed way of doing things. The old view of social problems, that is the extent to which individuals need help in overcoming difficulties, no longer seems relevant in this context. The present mood is one of redistributing resources, of changing the rules of the game, of righting the imbalance of power. This mood is reflected in the familiar expression, "We are living in a period of rapid social change."

This mood is different because it contrasts social change with individual change. Problems are looked at in terms of their roots in the social system, the organized way of doing things. In the words of the report of the Kerner Commission, the answer to racial unrest requires "new initiatives and experiments that can change the system of failure and frustration that now dominates the ghetto and weakens our society."[2] Those who are committed to social planning as a process by which society can resolve these problems are increasingly asking the question, "What does it mean to change the system, to change the rules of the game, to examine problems structurally?"

General objectives   This book attempts to develop some operational understanding of one such approach to problem solving, *social-structural change*. Although this concept is elaborated in Chapter 2, a brief summary of its meaning as implied in this analysis follows.

By social-structural change we mean alterations in the pattern of relationships which exist among people involved in a given situation. This involvement is called a *system of social relationships*. Such systems can be simple groups, such as a boys' club or a school classroom, or they can be as complex as a factory or a community. The pattern of relation-

---

1 Lee Rainwater, book review of "The Uses of Sociology," *American Sociological Review*, 33 (August 1968), 621f.

2 The National Advisory Commission on Civil Disorders, *Report of the National Advisory Commission on Civil Disorders* (New York: Bantam Books, 1968), p. 2.

ships among the individuals in such systems is called the *social structure*. It consists of the combination of *statuses* and *roles* which are peculiar to that system. Social-structural change consists of either a change in the combination of statuses or roles which make up the structure or a change in the type of people who occupy that structure.

The basic assumption underlying this analysis is that social-structural change can have a significant impact on the behavior or conditions of individuals which constitute a social problem of public importance.

The idea for this formulation was suggested by the work of the nineteenth-century French sociologist, Durkheim, who raised the level of consideration of human behavior from a preoccupation with individualism to a preoccupation with those patterns of behavior that derive from men acting in association.

> *One begins, Durkheim insisted, not with man, not with the individual...*
> *but with society. And society is not reducible to a vast aggregate of in-*
> *dividuals....*[3]

For Durkheim, society exists *sui generis*, and knowledge about society is not derivable from knowledge about individual behavior.

The specific focus of this book is not meant to be a panacea. Nor should it be construed, in a global sense, to involve changing the whole social system. However, it is one formulation of how to look for solutions to problems in human behavior in terms of the system of social relationships in which they occur.

Specific objectives   Specifically, our analysis will seek to answer two questions:

1. By what process are problems translated into social-structural terms?
2. What tools are available to the planner for structural intervention?

These objectives are a response to two frequent questions about the general concept of social structure as a point of intervention. On the one hand, the term is used indiscriminately to refer to any alteration in man's social environment, from the provision of individualized services to the enactment of legislation. In this sense, a plea for consideration of social-structural change as a new approach to problem solving meets with the natural response, "But isn't that what we are doing already?" Our analysis

3 Robert A. Nisbet, *Émile Durkheim* (Englewood Cliffs, N.J.: Prentice-Hall, Inc., 1965), p. 13.

will seek to answer the question by clarifying the concept of social structure and analyzing its application to problems in human behavior of current public interest.

The provision of a more delimited definition brings forth a question of method. When it is pointed out that structural change involves some direct alteration in peoples' patterns of social relationships, the question arises, "What techniques are available to the socially-oriented professions for bringing about such change?" We will answer this question by identifying the points of intervention in such systems of social relationships and the tools available for their change.

Underlying this analysis is an assumption about the type of role played by a planner. He is an individual who has direct access to policy-making bodies in government or voluntary organizations. He may be the executive officer of such an agency, or a staff member directly responsible to such an officer for planning new programs or making recommendations on questions of policy. Prototypes of such planners at the local community level are the mayor's assistant, the city planning staff of a municipality, or the planning staff of a direct service agency such as the welfare department, housing authority, department of public health, or board of education. Increasingly such planners are being found at the state and regional levels in human resources "super" agencies, regional development commissions, and budgeting arms of state and federal governments.

Limitations of scope   Because of the surge of interest in the subject of social structure and social change there is bound to be misunderstanding about the scope of this analysis. Certain questions immediately come to mind which will *not* be dealt with. For example, how desirable is social-structural change as a method of problem solving?

It is obvious that in some cases structural change may have unacceptable consequences. A classical example is the current controversy over black separatism. On the one hand, this movement to restructure communities in terms of their racial composition can result in stronger group identification and more effective political power for Blacks. On the other hand, it can polarize attitudes with regard to public resources and generate self-defeating conflict with similarly disadvantaged groups who, likewise, need additional resources for which black separatists strive.

The issue of the desirability of social-structural change with respect to any given problem will not be dealt with here. Our objective is simply to operationalize the approach to problem solving so that its merits can be considered.

Another question which naturally arises is, how effective are structural changes in resolving a given problem? For example, it could be argued that mentally-ill persons may experience a reduction in their symptoms by being integrated into communities in which their job status and family status would be less threatening. But, in the absence of more intensive attention to personality structure, how significant a difference would such special social structures make?

To the extent that the cases presented here are based on valid research, the question can be answered. However our objective is more modest. As a first step in the advancement of a new conceptual model for planning, we are concerned primarily with examining the nature of that model. It remains for later works to compare the results of this model with alternative approaches to problem solving. Therefore, in each case the focus of analysis is on the way people conceptualize problems rather than the efficacy of the particular solution.

A third subject which remains outside the scope of this analysis is the methods by which the planner develops the legitimacy and power to effect structural change once it has been identified. On this issue there already exists a more abundant literature.[4] In contrast, our purpose is to conceptualize the object of social change, to identify the types of goals to be achieved.

THE GROWING DEMAND FOR PLANNING MODELS

The subject of this analysis has considerable practical significance.

There is a growing acceptance of public responsibility for issues involving the social order. In the past, solutions to such problems as poverty, racism, inadequate housing, and even ill health have had to be justified in terms of a value preference for moral suasion and voluntary action.

One can easily trace the increasing assumption of responsibility for action on these matters by government at both the local and federal levels. In terms of the physical environment, public responsibility grew from a modest beginning in public housing into a more comprehensive attack on physical blight under urban renewal, and finally emerged as the socially oriented Model Cities Program. In relation to illness, private medical practice has evolved into group and institutional care and has been augmented by Medicare, Medicaid, and comprehensive health planning. Similar expansions can be seen in the field of education with

---

4 See, for example, Robert Morris and Robert H. Binstock, *Feasible Planning for Social Change* (New York: Columbia University Press, 1966); *Urban Government, A Reader in Administration*, rev. ed., ed. Edward C. Banfield (New York: The Free Press, 1969) for an introduction to this literature.

the establishment of Head Start programs, "community control" of public schools, and community colleges.

With this widening area of responsibility there has developed in each of these fields an interest in the community in terms of the social environment in which human needs arise. For example, the Model Cities Program is charged with a social as well as a physical renewal of the community; the medical-care field has broken out of the confines of the clinic and the hospital into a new form of practice—community health or social medicine; the field of education is examining educational policy in light of the needs of the urban community and not just an aggregate of students. These developments involve the search for a rationale for intervening into the social environment.

As a consequence, the professions which have been the guardians of the practice of social intervention have been pressed to re-examine their base of knowledge.

Two professions closely identified with efforts to shape communities for the enhancement of human welfare are city planning and social work. During the 1960s both professions attempted to formulate a definition of social planning that would provide a rationale for such intervention.[5] Yet both professions are seriously handicapped by the lack of a conceptualization of society as the basis for such a model of practice.

The profession of city planning, dominated as it has been by the disciplines of architecture and land economics, has been preoccupied with the physical development of cities, assuming that aesthetically pleasing buildings, smooth-flowing traffic, and segregated land use are the essential ingredients of a more liveable city. On the other hand, social work, dominated by the discipline of psychology, has been preoccupied with changing individuals, assuming that the aggregate of improved individuals is an improved society.

Unhappily, both lack a key element: a conceptual framework that focuses attention on society in terms of social organization and social processes as the object of analysis and change. While city planning appropriately emphasizes the environment as the object of practice it lacks a perspective of social organization as a crucial element in that environment. And while social work recognizes the importance of societal influences on human behavior, it lacks a perspective of environmental change as its concept of practice.

The response to increased public attention to issues of social change

5 See Bernard J. Frieden, "The Changing Prospects for Social Planning," *Journal of the American Institute of Planners*, **33** (September 1967), 311–23; and Alfred J. Kahn, "Social Science and the Conceptual Framework for Community Organization Research," in *Social Science Theory and Social Work Research*, ed. by Leonard S. Kogan (New York: National Association of Social Workers, 1960), pp. 64–80.

takes yet another form. There has been a proliferation in recent years of new training programs at the graduate level in universities around the country—both inside and outside the established socially-oriented professions—in which attempts are made to identify the knowledge and provide the training necessary for planned social change. Some schools of city planning are instituting new concentrations in "social policy planning." Schools of social work are expanding and upgrading their programs in community organization and social planning.[6] One state university has established an entire college devoted to professional education in methods of enhancing the relationship between man and his environment. New centers for the study of public policy and its formulation are emerging.[7]

The subject of this book, therefore, is of considerable importance. Not only has public policy come to favor social planning, but the professions responsible for formulating methodologies, and universities responsible for training practitioners are looking for a new concept of practice which deals with the way in which man's problems are rooted in the social order in which he lives.

A REVIEW OF ATTEMPTS TO CONCEPTUALIZE SOCIAL PLANNING

In recent years there has been a marked increase in the literature on the general subject of planned social change. However, much of this literature focuses on the process of planning or the effectuation of plans, alternately referred to as the decision-making process.

For example, Morris and Binstock provide a careful analysis of the planning process in terms of matching the control over sources of influence with the types of resistance to change encountered by the planner.[8] They do not purport to discuss the subject matter of social planning. Similarly, Roland L. Warren focuses primarily on the varying conditions under which different change strategies may be successful as

---

6 See Arnold Gurin, et al., Community Organization Curriculum in Graduate Social Work Education: Report and Recommendations (New York: Council on Social Work Education, 1970); Arnold Gurin and Robert Perlman, Community Organization and Social Planning, (New York: John Wiley and Sons, Inc. and Council on Social Work Education, 1970); Joan Ecklein and Armand Lauffer, Community Organizers and Social Planners: A Casebook (New York: John Wiley and Sons, Inc. and Council on Social Work Education, 1970); Jack Rothman and Wyatt Jones, A New Look at Field Instruction: Education for Application of Practice Skills in Community Organization and Social Planning (New York: Association Press and Council on Social Work Education, 1970); Ralph Kramer and Harry Specht, Readings in Community Organization Practice (Englewood Cliffs, N. J.: Prentice-Hall, Inc., 1970).

7 Examples can be found in schools of city planning from the Massachusetts Institute of Technology, the University of California at Berkeley, and the University of North Carolina at Chapel Hill, to the College of Human Development at Pennsylvania State University, and the Public Policy Program at Harvard University.

8 Morris and Binstock, Feasible Planning for Social Change.

well as the organizational instrumentalities through which change takes place.[9] Even the more recent work by Alfred J. Kahn is primarily focused on the process rather than the substance of social planning. Kahn's premise is that

> *Unlike the economic planner who...can point to the "system" in which he intervenes, there is no clearly or even vaguely bounded social system which is a field apart for the social planner and in which the results of intervention are observable.*[10]

However, the question with which this volume deals and consequently the literature to be reviewed can be couched in these terms: What constitutes the subject matter of social planning? With what issues does it deal? What are the social variables brought to bear on the search for solutions to a given problem? To note this distinction is not to depreciate the importance of strategies of social change. But, as Talcott Parsons observed, "To have such a theory (of social change) it is necessary to know what it is that changes."[11]

The relevant literature that deals with defining the subject of social planning is drawn primarily from four fields of practice involved in articulating the nature and scope of social intervention. These fields are: (1) social work, (2) delinquency prevention, (3) community mental health, and (4) city planning.[12]

An important qualification should be kept in mind while reviewing this literature. There are undoubtedly instances where practice deviates from the instances depicted in the literature reviewed here. However, our primary interest involves knowledge building. The pursuit of such an interest requires that the material under study be articulated in a form that is communicable, replicable, and subject to verification.

Social work   An examination of basic documents in social work theory reveals that the mainstream of social work practice in this country has stemmed from analytical individualism. While there have been periods in which social reform was considered a major preoccupation,

9 Roland L. Warren, *Types of Purposive Social Change at the Community Level* (Waltham, Mass.: Brandeis University, 1965), and "The Interorganizational Field as a Focus for Investigation," *Administrative Science Quarterly*, 12 (December 1967) 396–419.

10 Alfred J. Kahn, *Theory and Practice of Social Planning* (New York: Russell Sage Foundation, 1969), p. 27.

11 Talcott Parsons, *The Structure of Social Action* (Glencoe, Ill.: The Free Press, 1949), p. 450.

12 Social work and city planning are confusing terms in that they refer both to professional methodologies applied within programmatic fields (e.g. mental health and urban renewal) as well as to organized activities in their own right (e.g. casework services and master planning). It is in the latter sense that they are employed here.

the dominant model of practice since World War I has been social casework. Social work's failure to recognize society as an object of study and practice in and of itself is of course related to the professions' origins in nineteenth-century charity work and its theoretical basis in Freudian psychology.[13]

In this context, attempts to deal with the notion of society have tended to represent extrapolations from theory of or experience in dealing with individuals. This tendency has made difficult the recognition of the origins of problems in the way society is organized, and the recognition of social structure as an object of practice. As late as 1950, Elizabeth Herzog characterized the main thrust of social work as "adjustments consciously effected, individual by individual, between men and their social environments."[14]

There did emerge in the 1950s a recognition that social and cultural forces affect the nature of problems treated by social workers on an individual basis. This recognition was given expression in the work of Stein and Cloward.[15] However, it did not lead to a new conceptualization of practice based on a theory of social intervention. Stein and Cloward's work can be characterized as an attempt to enlarge the caseworker's perspective of his client by the inclusion of sociocultural factors into individualized treatment.

Practitioners attuned to the importance of the social environment as well as to psychodynamics will find in this volume significant keys to environmental stresses against which the client's reactions may be evaluated....[16]

Within the field of social work, interest in social planning or social intervention has arisen out of that branch of the profession known as community organization. However, its minority status in the field has made difficult the establishment of an independent and appropriate theoretical base. Since the primary business of social work was thought to be individual change rather than social change, community organization was seen primarily as an ancillary method. Its purpose was to mobilize community resources for the provision of services deemed necessary by social workers in the treatment of individual cases. Planning, therefore, was concerned with achieving "a progressively more effective adjustment between social welfare resources and needs."[17] Helen L. Witmer's

13 Harold L. Wilensky and Charles N. Lebeaux, *Industrial Society and Social Welfare* (New York: Russell Sage Foundation, 1958), pp. 325–34.
14 Elizabeth G. Herzog, "What Social Casework Wants of Social Science Research," *American Sociological Review,* 16 (February 1951), 68–73.
15 Herman D. Stein and Richard A. Cloward, *Social Perspectives on Behavior, A Reader in Social Science for Social Work and Related Professions* (Glencoe, Ill.: The Free Press, 1958).
16 *Ibid.,* p. xiif.
17 Kahn, *Social Science,* p. 67.

careful analysis of social work as a social institution reflects this traditional view.[18]

It is quite understandable, therefore, that community organization did not achieve equal status as an educational concentration with the other methods of social work until 1962.[19]

The theoretical difficulties encountered along the way are well documented by Kahn in a landmark analysis of attempts to conceptualize community organization practice.[20] One of the early dominant themes which underlay attempts to define community organization as an independent discipline was that of Pray.

The problems, then, with which social work deals are not problems of social structure, as such, nor of individual personality, as such.... They are problems which people find in the actual process of adjustment to each other or to any part or aspect of their environment.[21]

This view, which was influential for a decade, typifies the continuing failure to grasp social structure as the object of social intervention. Community organization is seen in the context of working with individual citizens, and communities appear nothing more than the sum total of individual adjustments.

The 1950s were characterized by an uneasiness on the part of writers and practitioners to limit the focus of community organization to social welfare services, in light of the growing size and complexity of America's urban social problems. One of the most significant works in this period was that of Murray C. Ross. His was the first attempt to derive from the social sciences a theoretical basis for community organization.[22] Yet his primary interest in community integration rested heavily on a social psychological model of intervention. His notion of changing communities was to enhance the participation of individuals in group processes. He argued that involving individuals in group efforts of identifying needs, ranking them, finding resources, and taking action, will result in new attitudes of integration and social solidarity.[23]

18 Helen L. Witmer, *Social Work, An Analysis of a Social Institution* (New York: Holt, Rinehart & Winston, Inc., 1942) p. 39.
19 Arnold Gurin and Robert Perlman, "An Overview of the Community Organization Curriculum Development Project and its Recommendations," *Education for Social Work* (Spring 1969), p. 38.
20 Kahn, *Social Science*.
21 *Ibid.*, p. 66.
22 Murray C. Ross, *Community Organization Theory and Principles* (New York: Harper & Row, Publishers, 1955).
23 Kahn, *Social Science*, pp. 68f.

Ross's model of change represents a projection of behavior in face-to-face primary relationships onto the functioning of society. Of such a view Kahn states:

> Some writers overuse the therapist analogy in describing the community organization role. Their acknowledgement of this, as in the case of Ross, does not erase the fact that it is a natural consequence of inappropriate emphasis on the similarity between community organization, group work, and casework.[24]

Kahn's overall assessment of the development of community organization practice during this period was both discouraging and promising. It was discouraging because it acknowledged an absence in existing social work writing of an adequate theoretical base for practitioners interested in the community. It was promising, because for the first time a social work theoretician recognized that a sociologistic perspective must be the central focus of such a theory.

> . . . The social sciences may soon be in a position to provide for community organization, much as psychoanalysis did for casework, some of the key organizing concepts necessary for adequate formulation of the much sought after theory.[25]

It was not until the 1960s that such a conceptualization emerged as an outgrowth of experimentation in the control of juvenile delinquency.

Delinquency prevention   The field of corrections, those remedial programs dealing with adult and juvenile crime, has had a more sociological orientation than other fields we have discussed. The history of various theories relating delinquency to aspects of social structure and culture is well documented.[26] However, practice has primarily emphasized individual change, either through training programs or counseling.

Cloward and Ohlin introduced a new and significant approach based on social-structural change. Their opportunity theory led to the program of prevention and control known as Mobilization for Youth in New York City.[27]

---

24 *Ibid.*, p. 76.
25 *Ibid.*, p. 65.
26 Alfred J. Kahn, "From Delinquency Treatment to Community Development" in *The Uses of Sociology*, eds. Paul F. Lazarsfeld, William H. Sewell, and Harold L. Wilensky (New York: Basic Books, 1967), pp. 477–506.
27 *A Proposal for the Prevention and Control of Delinquency by Expanding Opportunities* (New York: Mobilization for Youth, Inc., 1961), pp. 41ff.

Utilizing Robert K. Merton's theory of deviant behavior,[28] Cloward and Ohlin argued that juvenile delinquency is a response to the lack of opportunities—in the form of occupational and educational channels—for lower-class youth to achieve the culturally defined goals of material success in our society[29] This analysis implies that the sources of the difficulty lie in the social position of delinquent individuals within our society, and the accompanying deficiency of resources and legitimate means to success of such a position. It suggests a strategy of social-structural change.

> If the possibilities for a conventional adjustment are restricted or absent, the likelihood is that the offender, no matter how favorably motivated, will continue to engage in nonconforming behavior. Thus we must concern ourselves with expanding opportunities for conventional behavior. Our program is designed to enlarge opportunities for conformity and so to combat a major source of delinquent behavior among young people.[30]

However, the remedies elaborated in the initial proposal for this program constitute attempts not to change the opportunity structure, but to change individuals by better equipping them to fit into the existing opportunity structure. The approach is called "increasing the capacity to utilize opportunity" and it consists of a series of programs to help lower-class youth acquire the necessary skills, attitudes, and aspirations for successful employment.

> We emphasize the fact, however, that merely providing new opportunities may not alleviate delinquency if youngsters are not also helped to exploit these opportunities. We noted that people who are denied access to various social resources soon lose the capacity to make use of them. Indeed, they may even develop organized patterns of living which become barriers to the utilization of opportunity. The problem is not that they are undersocialized or incompletely socialized, but, rather, that they are differently socialized. We suggest, therefore, that program forms must be evolved which will permit us to intervene in arresting these self-defeating models of behavior.[31]

The exception to this general approach is a community organization program designed to promote among neighborhood residents the aspirations for and the ability to seek social change.

28 Robert K. Merton, *Social Theory and Social Structure* (New York: The Free Press, 1968) pp. 185–249.
29 Richard A. Cloward and Lloyd E. Ohlin, *Delinquency and Opportunity* (Glencoe, Ill.: The Free Press, 1960), p. 78.
30 *A Proposal for the Prevention and Control of Delinquency by Expanding Opportunities, op. cit.,* p. 45.
31 *Ibid.,* p. 89.

Opportunities for collective social action should be incorporated into any large-scale delinquency program. We make this argument because we believe that a feeling of alienation from the larger society is a fundamental dynamic in much collective delinquent behavior. If opportunities for the constructive expression of alienation can be organized and employed, the problem of delinquency can be correspondingly reduced. The task is to direct the expression of alienation against the social structure which is its cause and to discourage its expression in delinquent acts. In this way, the discontented may help to alter the very inequalities which oppress them.[32]

In this formulation of practice, the Mobilization for Youth program is directed at social-structural change, however, only in an indirect way. Its goal is to gird lower class residents to fight their own battles to change the social structure, stopping short of prescribing aspects of social structure which need changing.[33] Thus, though a social problem is conceptualized in social-structural terms, its solution falls short of direct, planned structural change.

However, during the years following the inception of Mobilization for Youth there emerged even in that program, a more direct relationship between organizing activities and structural change. For example, Brager and Specht argued that poverty is in fact a result, not of insufficient skill on the part of individuals, but of the maldistribution of resources which arises from the imbalance of power in the community.[34] Efforts to organize the poor into solidary political groups were then seen as efforts to change the power structure of the community.

To the extent that the results of such efforts become institutionalized beyond social action episodes—such as the unionization of workers within the industrial system—organizing the poor would constitute a social-structural change. Such a conceptual framework is beginning to appear in the professional literature and the curricula of schools of social work and represents a new conceptual development during the decade since Kahn's original analysis in 1960.

Community mental health[35]   Within the various mental health professions there has evolved a widespread interest in what is called

---

32 *Ibid.*, p. 69.

33 For further illustration, see Warren C. Haggstrom, "The Power of the Poor," in *Mental Health of the Poor*, eds. Frank Reissman, Jerome Cohen, and Arthur Pearl (New York: The Free Press, 1964), pp. 205–23.

34 George A. Brager and Harry Specht, "Social Action by the Poor: Prospects, Problems, and Strategies," in *Community Action Against Poverty* eds. George A. Brager and Francis P. Purcell (New Haven: College and University Press, 1967), pp. 133–51.

35 In the literature under review in this section, there is a tendency to use the terms community mental health programs, community psychiatry, and social psychiatry interchangeably. While there are recognizable differences in the phenomena referred to, they are not substantive in this discussion. Therefore the general term community mental health will be used throughout.

community mental health. This umbrella concept has not resulted from any thorough and systematic analysis of the relationship between social structure and mental illness. Rather, it has grown out of widely differing perceptions of the limitations of existing mental health programs.

Stemming from its theoretical roots in psychology and its practice experience in the psychiatric treatment of individuals, community mental health constitutes an effort on the part of the mental health professionals to deal more systematically with mental illness. In this sense, the community mental health movement represents an attempt to extrapolate knowledge about mentally healthy conditions in the community from knowledge of individual pathology. The problems in such a procedure were pointed out long ago by Durkheim: one cannot deduce knowledge about social causation from knowledge about individual behavior.[36]

H. Warren Dunham has summarized the conceptual difficulties of the community mental health movement by differentiating among its varied but rarely explicated meanings.[37]

Group therapy, when it involves groups indigenous to the patient, such as the family, does involve the system of social relationships in which the individual is embedded. However, the object of change in such a technique is the individual—his responses to the social processes of the group—rather than the structure of the group.

Community mental health sometimes refers to the attempt to prevent mental breakdown through early detection and public education about the causes of mental illness. This meaning is reflected in Alexander H. Leighton's discussion of social psychiatry as the extension of psychiatric knowledge into the social groups of which the mentally-ill person is a member.[38] Thus the psychiatrist works in schools, factories, and agencies of government to identify mental disturbances at their onset and to enhance the ability of "caretakers" to prevent deterioration and facilitate recovery. Such a function does not represent any essential departure from psychologism as a perspective of causation. At best it increases understanding of mental disorders and tolerance of deviant behavior among members of the social system with whom the afflicted person must interact.

Still another use of the term implies the organization and use of

---

36 Émile Durkheim, *The Elementary Forms of Religious Life,* trans. Joseph Ward Swain (London: George Allen & Unwin Ltd., 1915) p. 16.

37 H. Warren Dunham, "Community Psychiatry: The Newest Therapeutic Bandwagon," in *The Sociology of Mental Disorders,* ed. S. Kirson Weinberg (Chicago: Aldine Publishing Co., 1967), pp. 315–20. For a similar categorization, see Alexander H. Leighton, John A. Clausen, and Robert N. Wilson, eds., *Explorations in Social Psychiatry* (New York: Basic Books, Inc., Publishers, 1957), p. 4, footnote.

38 Alexander H. Leighton, *An Introduction to Social Psychiatry* (Springfield, Ill.: Charles C Thomas, Publisher, 1960).

hospital care vis-à-vis patient care in the community.[39] Attention to the therapeutic aspects of community life does recognize the importance of social-structural variables in achieving mental health. However, treatment is still focused on the ill person rather than the creation of new forms of social life to resolve intra-psychic conflict.

The most tenuous use of the term community mental health focuses on the societal functions that produce mental illness and represents a relatively uncharted area of conceptualization. It is in this sense that the movement is most vulnerable to theoretical criticism. Attempts to locate the etiology of mental illness in the community and to apply treatment to collectivities requires a theoretical perspective which is clearly based on social structure and social processes rather than psychodynamics.[40]

The implication of this last meaning has led S. Kirson Weinberg to coin a new phrase—psychiatric sociology—to clarify its distinctiveness from the more popular connotations of the term community mental health.[41] Psychiatric sociology represents a clear theoretical departure for it uses a sociologistic framework for viewing the phenomenon of mental illness. According to this perspective mental illness stems not from weaknesses in the personality, but from intolerable stresses created by the social environment. Weinberg explains this position as follows:

> ...The predominant sociological position has emphasized that, despite the significance of early experiences in personality formation, stresses in all stages of the person's life cycle may affect this instability and mental disorder. For example, during World War II some soldiers who had relatively stable childhoods experienced neurotic and even psychotic breakdowns which implied that even relatively stable persons could break down under severe stress....The sociological position that has pointed to the stresses in subsequent life has also encouraged inquiries into the effects of peers, the school, the work situation, marriage, and retirement in senescence upon disordered behavior.[42]

However, having raised the perspective of causation from an individual to a societal level, Weinberg fails to do the same for a model of practice. He sees the sociology of mental disorders applied primarily

39 See particularly Howard E. Freeman and Ozzie G. Simmons, *The Mental Patient Comes Home* (New York: John Wiley & Sons, Inc., 1963); and Erving Goffman, *Asylums* (Chicago: Aldine Publishing Co., 1962).

40 H. Warren Dunham, *op.cit.*, pp. 317f; and Howard E. Freeman and Wyatt C. Jones, *Social Problems: Their Causes and Control* (Chicago: Rand-McNally & Co., 1970).

41 S. Kirson Weinberg, "Psychiatric Sociology: The Sociology of Mental Disorders," in *The Sociology of Mental Disorders, Analyses and Readings in Psychiatric Sociology*, ed. S. Kirson Weinberg (Chicago: Aldine Publishing Co., 1967), pp. 3–8.

42 *Ibid.*, p. 4.

through the vehicle of social psychiatry. "The pervasive definition of social psychiatry pertains to social action and subsumes 'community psychiatry,' 'preventive psychiatry' and social change of psychiatric institutions."[43]

Although he makes reference to social action, Weinberg does not develop it as a model of practice. Instead he focuses his elaboration of social psychiatry on the treatment and care of disordered persons utilizing knowledge derived from the social sciences integrated with the skills of the psychiatrist.

> *Thus, one pervasive version of social psychiatry, as defined by Wilmer and Leighton, is that of an eclectic and applied discipline used by the psychiatrist in his particular role. Ruesh has regarded social psychiatry in these terms as "a hybrid discipline which attempts to integrate and apply the knowledge derived from the social sciences with the skills of the psychiatrist."[44]*

It is difficult to see how this function differs from that of the social caseworker, a model long familiar to the profession of social work.

In terms of the assumptions underlying this analysis, social psychiatry is not the practice model most appropriate to a sociological interpretation of mental illness. The preferred model is social planning which attempts to alter aspects of social structure and redirect social processes. It remains to be seen whether such a model can be developed within the field of mental health.

City planning   In the field of city planning, serious efforts to reorient practice toward social intervention are fairly recent. They have been spurred in the 1960s by the recognition that the development of cities is being hampered in large part by the social problems with which urban renewal as a remedy is relatively ineffective. The advent of the War on Poverty and the Model Cities Program has given substance to these efforts.[45]

Attempts by city planners to conceptualize social planning have tended to take three different forms: (1) those equating social planning with the development and deployment of social services, (2) those equating social planning with comprehensiveness, and (3) those equating social planning with advocacy of the interests of disadvantaged segments of the population.

43 *Ibid.*, p. 5.
44 *Ibid.*, p. 5.
45 Frieden, "The Changing Prospects for Social Planning," p. 33.

Defining social planning as the development of health, welfare, recreation, education, and related services to meet the needs of individuals grows out of the social welfare traditions of this country. As noted by Herbert J. Gans, "In its American usage the term social planning comes from social welfare, where it refers to interagency coordination of social work programs."[46] This line of development began with the association between social workers, city planners, and housing officials in connection with the problems of disadvantaged persons encountered in public housing and urban renewal programs. These problems were conceptualized as unmet needs for social welfare services.[47]

This view is expressed by Harvey S. Perloff who sees as the central issue in social planning the adequacy of public, private, and voluntary social services—in health, welfare, and education—for the population at risk in a given area.[48] Such a formulation is identical to the familiar social work model of planning, balancing social welfare resources to meet social welfare needs.

The second view of social planning, characterized by comprehensiveness, represents an expansion of the first. It reflects a greater sophistication regarding the complexity of the city, as well as the proliferation in the past decade of planning functions in specific areas of urban life. It is expressed by Melvin M. Webber in the following excerpt:

> We are coming to comprehend the city as an extremely complex social system, only some aspects of which are expressed as physical buildings or as locational arrangements. As the parallel, we are coming to understand that each aspect lies in a reciprocal causal relation to all others, such that each is defined by, and has meaning only with respect to, its relations to all others.
>
> As one result of this broadened conception of the city system, we can no longer speak of the physical city versus the social city or the economic city or the political city or the intellectual city . . . if distinguishable at all, the distinction is that of constituent component, as with metals comprising an alloy.[49]

Comprehensiveness represents an attempt to put the analytical pieces of the city back together again, to re-establish a whole. It is social in the sense that it attempts to subject the goals established in areas of

46 Herbert J. Gans, *People and Plans* (New York: Basic Books, Inc., Publishers, 1968), p. 72.
47 See Elizabeth Wood, *The Small Hardcore* (New York: Citizens' Housing and Planning Council of New York, Inc. 1957); and *Working Together for Urban Renewal, A Guide on Why, When, and How Social Welfare Agencies and Urban Renewal Agencies Should Work Together* (Chicago: National Association of Housing and Redevelopment Officials, 1958).
48 Harvey S. Perloff, "New Directions in Social Planning," *Journal of the American Institute of Planners*, 31 (November 1965) 297–304.
49 Melvin M. Webber, "Comprehensive Planning and Social Responsibility," in *Urban Planning and Social Policy*, eds. Bernard J. Frieden and Robert Morris (New York: Basic Books, Inc., Publishers, 1968), p. 14.

specialized planning—health, transportation, social welfare, economic development, or housing—to a set of higher criteria, namely their effect on the needs of people, their relative contribution to achieving a more livable city.

While highly desirable in practice, the concept of comprehensiveness is very difficult in theory. To Gans, such a notion is operationally impossible. Since all goals affect at least a portion of the society, all goals are social.[50] Gans' solution is to use the term *societal* to refer to any goal adopted by the government for the society, and to reserve the term *social* to refer to all noneconomic, nonphysical programs designed to achieve societal goals.

Desirable as such integration may be, the concept of comprehensiveness does not lend itself to the development of a technology of social planning. It runs counter to the history of man's success in gaining control over his environment. As John Kenneth Galbraith has pointed out, progress in science and technology is achieved through the sequential breakdown of human experience, albeit abstractions, into analytical components which can be understood and mastered.[51] It is in this sense that the conceptualization of social planning as the comprehensive "putting together" of the whole city detracts from the need to develop a more precise understanding of the social structures and social processes that affect man's life in urban communities.

A third distinct meaning of social planning is implied in the now familiar concept of advocacy planning proposed by Paul Davidoff and others.[52] Advocacy planning refers essentially to the relationship between city planners and the conflicting value-sets or vested interests of different subgroups in the community. It is operationalized in terms of the alignment of planners with the interests of those disadvantaged subgroups that heretofore have not been in a position to articulate their needs in the process of community decision-making. The objective of such planning is to effect a redistribution of public resources from the most advantaged to the least advantaged sectors of the urban community.

In this respect, advocacy planning is very much like community organization within the field of social work. As such it is not a concept of social planning for it does not lead to a definition or delimiting of the subject of change. It refers to the process of achieving changes, whatever they may be.

No discussion of the perspectives of social planning on the part of city planners would be complete without reference to the work of Gans.

50 Gans, *People and Plans*, p. 85.

51 John Kenneth Galbraith, *The New Industrial State* (New York: The New American Library, Inc., 1968), p. 24.

52 Paul Davidoff, "Advocacy and Pluralism in Planning," *Journal of the American Institute of Planners*, 31 (November 1965), 331–38.

As a trained sociologist and city planner, Gans' analysis of problems of the city conveys an awareness of social systems and their structures. However, most of his writings can be characterized as a critique of existing practice in the field of city planning and social planning, rather than as a formulation of what properly constitutes social planning.

His best known work, *The Urban Villagers*, represents the use of a social systems conceptualization to understand the life of an urban working-class neighborhood.[53] However his prescriptions for change are not particularly structural. They are more in keeping with the proposals of Mobilization for Youth, which he calls *guided mobility*.[54]

Gans' conceptualization of social planning can be seen most clearly in his discussion of the relationship between the *potential environment* and the *effective environment*.[55]

> *The basic conception to be argued here is: the physical environment is relevant to behavior insofar as this environment effects the social system and culture of the people involved or as it is taken up into their social system. Between the physical environment and empirically observable human behavior, there exists a social system and a set of cultural norms which define and evaluate portions of the physical environment relevant to the lives of people involved and structure the way people would use (and react to) this environment in their daily lives.*

In applying these concepts to practice, Gans points out that a park proposed by a planner is only a potential environment. "The social system and culture of the people who would use it determine to what extent the park becomes an *effective environment*."[56] The implication here is that the job of the social planner is to create a better match between potential environments and effective environments, that is, to develop facilities in the city in such a way that they will fit into the social systems and culture of the people for whose use and benefit they are intended.

This formulation tends to create a passive role for the social planner; he reacts to, rather than initiates change. He molds innovation to fit existing social structures, rather than changes structures themselves. However, it does place the discussion of social planning in the realm of concepts having to do with social systems, of which social-structural change is a part. It serves therefore as a fitting conceptual bridge to the central task of this book.

53 Herbert J. Gans, *The Urban Villagers* (New York: The Free Press, 1962).
54 Herbert J. Gans, "Social and Physical Planning for the Elimination of Urban Poverty," in *Urban Planning and Social Policy*, eds. Frieden and Morris, pp. 43–53.
55 Gans, *People and Plans*, pp. 4–12.
56 *Ibid.*, p. 6.

Summary   This review of the professional literature has identified three basic ways of conceptualizing the subject matter of social planning: (1) the provision of organized services to individuals to help them overcome deficiencies in their environment, or handicaps to their advancement within the present system, (2) the integration of all programs designed to improve living conditions in the city in terms of some overriding consideration of their enhancement of the welfare of the residents involved, and (3) the equipping of disadvantaged groups with the technology and organization to exert pressure on centers of power for a more favorable distribution of resources.

From the point of view of this analysis, the first conceptualization is not structural because it is focused essentially on individuals as the unit of analysis and the object of change. The second conceptualization, while it may certainly involve structural change, is too global to provide an analytical framework with which to identify the peculiar characteristics of social-structural change. The last conceptualization is directed at the process of achieving social-structural change, but does not shed light on the substance of that change.

In the next chapter, the concept of social-structural change will be elaborated as an alternative to these formulations.

Chapter 2

WHAT IS SOCIAL-STRUCTURAL CHANGE?

This chapter examines the concepts social structure and social change as they are used most frequently in the literature. Its purpose is to develop criteria which can be used for selecting cases of change involving social structures.

This effort of conceptual clarification involves two considerations. First, we will examine the distinguishing characteristics of structural phenomena and second we will delineate the nature of social change as it is used in this book.

DISTINGUISHING CHARACTERISTICS OF STRUCTURAL PHENOMENA

The notion of social-structural change, which is the subject of this book, is rooted in the elementary ideas of one of the founders of modern sociology, Émile Durkheim. It is appropriate, therefore, to begin the search for clarification of social structure with Durkheim's central ideas.

The contribution of Durkheim that has primary relevance for this subject is his discussion of the nature of a social fact.[1] For Durkheim there are two distinctive characteristics of a social fact:

1. It is a property of a social aggregate or group, not its individual members.
2. It is capable of exercising control over the individual.

> *A social fact is every way of acting, fixed or not, capable of exercising on the individual an external constraint; or again, every way of acting which is general throughout a given society, while at the same time existing in its own right independent of its individual manifestations.*[2]

Parsons has paraphrased Durkheim. "The 'social' element is that element of the total concrete reality of human action in society which is attributable to the fact of association in collective life."[3]

As Durkheim intended, these two criteria delimit the field of sociology in general rather than the phenomenon of social structure in particular. They serve, therefore, as necessary but not sufficient conditions for specifying structural phenomena. They do not answer the encompassing question: Which of all the various social facts or characteristics of a a system of social relations refer specifically to social structure?

To answer this question requires an examination of the way in which the term social structure has been used by sociologists since the time of Durkheim. This task is not made easy by the fact that sociologists have tended to use the term in an indiscriminate and comprehensive sense, that is to refer to the total range of social facts.[4]

In an effort to delineate the meaning of social structure, therefore, we will trace its progressive specification by three writers, Robert K. Merton, Ralph Linton, and Talcott Parsons. The work of these men probably accounts for the most widely recognized meanings of this concept.

Arrangement   The term arrangement probably best conveys in nontechnical language the central meaning of the concept social structure as used by most sociologists. It is the term that best describes Merton's early attempts to differentiate social structure from other social facts, as conveyed in the following excerpt.

---

1 Emile Durkheim, *The Rules of Sociological Method,* trans. Sara Solovay and John H. Mueller, 8th ed. (New York: The Free Press, 1964).

2 *Ibid.,* p. 13.

3 Talcott Parsons, *The Structure of Social Action,* p. 363.

4 See for example the introduction by George Catland in Durkheim, *The Rules of Sociological Method,* p. xvii.

>...*The salient environment of individuals can be usefully thought of as involving the cultural structure, on the one hand, and the social structure, on the other....In this connection, cultural structure may be defined as that organized set of normative values governing behavior which is common to members of a designated society or group. And by social structure is meant that organized set of social relationships in which members of a society or group are variously implicated.*[5]

For the most part, Merton uses for his referent of an "organized set of social relationships" the hierarchical arrangement of people according to social class. This is the manifestation of social structure that is of primary interest to him in explaining the phenomenon of deviant behavior.

Merton further clarifies the concept of social structure by introducing, albeit briefly, the notion of social system to imply the total social context in which action takes place.

>*Owing to their objectively disadvantaged position in the group as well as to distinctive personality configurations, some individuals are subjected more than others to the strains arising from the discrepancy between cultural goals and effective access to their realization. They are consequently more vulnerable to deviant behavior. In some proportion of cases, again dependent upon the control-structure of the group, these departures from institutional norms are socially rewarded by "successful" achievement of goals. But these deviant ways of achieving the goals occur within social systems. The deviant behavior consequently effects not only the individuals who first engage in it, but in some measure it also effects other individuals with whom they are inter-related in the system.*[6]

On the basis of these two observations from Merton's writing, it is possible to develop a more orderly picture of the various aspects of social situations, or social facts as Durkheim calls them. The total situation can be considered the *social system*. Within the system there is a set of prescribed goals and normative values shared by all which constitutes the *culture* of that system.[7] The members or individuals within the system are arranged in relation to each other, according to some hierarchical principle, and this arrangement is known as the *social structure*. There are, within a system, mechanisms or *institutions* that consist of a prescribed sequence of actions which perform some function

5 Robert K. Merton, *Social Theory and Social Structure*, p. 216.

6 *Ibid.*, pp. 233f.

7 It should be noted that Merton's use of culture in this sense is more restrictive than is customary among social scientists. Anthropologists such as Linton tend to use the term comprehensively to mean all social behavior that is learned. See Ralph Linton, *The Study of Man* (New York: Appleton-Century-Crofts, 1936).

for the system, for example, the use of rewards and punishment to achieve social control.

These distinctive concepts provide a basis for sorting out different aspects of a social situation for analysis. They all may be said to control or influence the behavior of members of a social group, but obviously each is a distinct type or source of such influence.

Status and role   In his discussion of reference groups, Merton introduces a more precise definition of structure, in contrast to the more general term, arrangement. He refers to the earlier work of Ralph Linton who argued that "two concepts—social status and social role—are fundamental to the description, and to the analysis, of a social structure."[8] Merton goes on to say:

> *By status, Linton meant a position in a social system occupied by designated individuals; by role, the behavioral enacting of the patterned expectations attributed to that position. Status and role, in these terms, are concepts serving to connect culturally defined expectations with the patterned behavior and relationship which comprise social structure.*[9]

Heretofore, the discussion has focused primarily on status as a characteristic of structural phenomena, the position of individuals in a system of social relationships. The introduction of the concept *role* establishes a behavioral dimension.

Linton discusses in more detail the relationship between status and role.

> *A status, as distinct from the individual who may occupy it, is simply a collection of rights and duties. . . .*

> *A role represents the dynamic aspect of a status. The individual is socially assigned to a status and occupies it with relation to other statuses. When he puts the rights and duties which constitute the status into effect, he is performing a role. Role and status are quite inseparable, and the distinction between them is of only academic interest. There are no roles without statuses or statuses without roles.*[10]

For Linton, the sum total of all status-roles within a society is what accounts for the pattern of reciprocal behavior between individuals or

8 Merton, *Social Theory and Social Structure*, p. 422.
9 *Ibid.*, p. 422.
10 Ralph Linton, *The Study of Man* (New York: Appleton-Century-Crofts, 1936), pp. 113f.

groups of individuals and which permits them to function together as a society.

There is an important distinction between Merton's concept of status and that of Linton. While Merton tends to see statuses in a hierarchical arrangement, Linton holds a more general view, that they may be arranged laterally as well. In Linton's perspective, statuses and roles represent the mutual adaptation of behavior on the part of component individuals, a division of labor to achieve mutual objectives. He continuously refers to reciprocity and congruity in the relationship between individuals in different statuses.

Similarly, in a social pattern such as that for the employer-employee relationship the statuses of employer and employee define what each has to know and do to put the pattern into operation. The employer does not need to know the techniques involved in the employee's labor, and the employee does not need to know the techniques for marketing or accounting.[11]

For Parsons, social structure has essentially the same meaning. The social structure is the combination of roles assigned to the various actors in a system of social interaction.

The differentiation of the social system may then be treated under two main headings. First, it is a system of differentiated roles. The types of which it is composed, how they are distributed within the social system, and how integrated with each other must be analyzed. This is what we mean by the social structure in the narrower sense of the term. Secondly, however, given the role structure, we must analyze the processes of distribution of "moveable" elements as between statuses and roles.[12]

Parsons likens the relationship between roles and functions relative to a social system to the relationship between organs and functions relative to an organism.

Like Linton, Parsons does not make a clear distinction between role and status. He uses the term status to refer to a position within the social structure. His reference to the distribution of rights or rewards as a characteristic of the social structure is consistent with the meaning attributed to the concept status by Linton. He usually uses the two terms conjunctively. However role is his primary concept for defining structure.

Parsons' view is similar to Linton's in another respect. He does not see structures as necessarily hierarchical. Hierarchical arrangements

11 *Ibid.,* p. 114.
12 Talcott Parsons, *The Social System* (Glencoe, Ill.: The Free Press, 1951), p. 114.

result from the distribution of roles in a system. When there is a "scarcity" in a given role, there is not room for an infinite number of actors in that role.

> *There seem to be essentially two types of these. One is the type of role which is near the "top" in a scale of responsibility or prestige or both—e.g., there can be only one President of the United States at a time—the other is the type of role which is extremely specialized in other respects—hence there are severe limitations on the "market" for the relevant products or services. An example would be the role of theoretical physicist.[13]*

The new element in Parsons' model stems from his recognition of the variation in shape and substance of social structures which results from the distribution and clustering of roles in a given social system.

> *We have noted that this distribution of role types is itself the basic structure of the social system as a system. This structure is described by the answers to such questions as of what types of roles is it made up, in what proportions and how distributed in "clusters"?[14]*

To Parsons the basic components of any social system are roles. The social structure of that system consists of the peculiar combination of roles and their distribution throughout the system. In such a scheme, Parsons can conceive of an infinite number of permutations and combinations of roles or structural elements, of sets or subsets to comprise the social structure.

In fact, he observes that every social structure has at least four types of role groupings. One is *kinship* which represents that cluster of statuses and roles derived from populations being grouped together on the basis of biological relatedness. A second substructure is that of *community*, which consists of those kinship units which share a common territory for residence. A third type of structure is the clustering of kinship units into *ethnic groups* based on common ancestry. And a fourth such structure is social *class*, a class being an aggregate of kinship units of approximately equal status in a stratified social system.

> *Therefore, we may say that membership in the four types of groupings, kinship, community, ethnic, and class, should characterize every individual actor in every society and such groupings should, with the requisite qualifications, be looked for as part of the structure of every society.[15]*

13 *Ibid.*, p. 116.
14 *Ibid.*, p. 116.
15 *Ibid.*, p. 173.

The point of interest in this latter discussion is that it is possible for a given social structure to have subgroupings of roles and statuses which can be thought of as substructures or partial structures.

Types of social structure   There remains the problem of clarifying the relationship between various terms used by Merton in referring to the general concept social structure. Throughout his analysis of deviant behavior, Merton uses the terms class structure, opportunity structure, power structure, and influence structure. In their usage they all imply an arrangement of people in a stratified social system. Upon closer inspection they all appear to be alternative types of such arrangements.

Merton's most frequent reference is to class structure. This practice probably results from the fact that social class represents the particular model of stratification relevant to his explanation of deviant behavior. Merton believes that for each social class there is a different degree of access to means for achieving success in our society. Since differential access to means for achieving success constitutes Merton's notion of opportunity structure, there is obviously a correlation in Merton's thinking between opportunity structure and class structure. Furthermore, recognizing that two frequently used indicators of social class, educational achievement and occupational status, constitute the primary means for achieving success according to Merton's theory, the opportunity structure must actually be synonymous with the class structure.

In discussing means of achieving success other than those available through the class structure, Merton introduces the concept of power structure. It is the racketeer, he says, who, having achieved success by society's standards, but through improper means, seeks to win legitimation by achieving a position of control within the power structure of the urban political machine.[16]

If we think of a political machine as a social system, then Merton's analysis implies a social structure based on one's ability to control the action of others which is different from a social structure based on social class. Merton goes on to point out that as the structure of opportunity changes, Italians were able to achieve success through the more legitimate means of professions and businesses. Thus, power becomes an alternative to social class as a basis for the hierarchical arrangement of people within a social system.

Still a third type of arrangement is reflected in Merton's description of a bureaucracy as a social system.[17] In such a system the hierarchical arrangement of individuals is on the basis of authority rather than social

16 Merton, *Social Theory and Social Structure*, pp. 246f.
17 *Ibid.*, p. 249.

class. Therefore it would be appropriate to refer to the social structure of the bureaucracy as an authority structure.

Thus the concept social structure can acquire a variety of prefixes depending on how one wishes to conceptualize the particular basis for the arrangement among individuals within a given social situation.

A summary definition of social structure   On the basis of this review of the theoretical literature, a summary definition of social structure can be established.

Social structure refers to the combination of statuses and accompanying roles in a system of social relationships.

There are two critical elements in this definition. One is the fact that social structure has meaning only with reference to a specified system of social interaction. A good deal of confusion can arise from considering an individual's various roles and statuses out of the context of a specific system. Without such context they may bear little sensible relationship to each other. It is the roles and statuses of a given system of social interaction which is the focal point for this analysis, rather than the roles and statuses pertaining to a given individual based on the variety of systems of social interaction in which he may participate.

The other critical element in this definition is the inseparability of the concepts role and status. They are really two distinct aspects of the same phenomenon, action in a system of social interaction. When we refer to roles, we mean the patterns of expected behavior which are associated with a given actor. Such behavioral patterns constitute functions in relation to the system of social interaction in which they are performed. On the other hand, statuses refer to the rights and obligations ascribed to these actors, and which facilitate or impede the enactment of the given roles. Thus, while the two terms refer to distinctly different characteristics, the effect of one is inseparable from the effect of the other.

The problem of reification   A frequent difficulty with concepts in the social sciences is the problem of *reification,* the tendency to equate conceptual abstractions of reality with an actual piece of reality. This problem plagued Durkheim, whose notion of social facts underlies this analysis. He was charged with positing the existence of social facts external to and independent of individual behavior. His resolution of this problem is instructive for us today.

Most sympathetic analysts agree that in his zeal to make a case for a sociologistic perspective of human behavior, Durkheim did tend to reify social facts in his early writings. However, as pointed out by Parsons, toward the end of his career Durkheim integrated the various aspects of man and society in his work, *L'education Morale*.[18]

True social control, Durkheim came to believe, does not result from the actor's being subjected to punishment for his violation of rules by some external authority. It results from the normative process in which the actor internalizes social norms which then determine the very goals he selects, *which prescribe acceptable actions before they happen*. Thus society is not separate from the individual, nor is the normative process external to him.

It is in this context that Durkheim's statements regarding individualism must be understood. Man is not a "self-sufficing, discrete, and self-stabilizing being."[19] "The fact is that he is not truly himself, he does not fully realize his own nature, except on the condition that he is involved in society."[20] "Moral life, in all its forms, is never met with except in society. It never varies except in relation to social conditions."[21]

Thus, Durkheim's view of society implies an abstraction of those elements of human behavior which can only be understood in terms of sociological concepts. As such it is no more a distortion of reality than the consideration of individuals apart from their social milieu.

> *It was not personality—not individuality—that Durkheim sought to drive out of sociological consideration; it was, rather, the artificial abstracted conception of individuality...which attributed to man's biological nature qualities which derived from the institutional and morale order of society.*[22]

Such a selective focus should not distract the reader from the larger fact of significance, that Durkheim demonstrated the existence of a social reality *sui generis*.

> *Nothing is more reasonable, then...that a belief or social practice may exist independently of its individual expressions. We clearly did not imply by this that society can exist without individuals, an obvious absurdity we might have been spared having attributed to us. But we did mean: (1) that this group formed by associated individuals has a reality of a different sort from each individual considered singly; (2) that collective*

18 Parsons, *The Structure of Social Action*, pp. 385f.
19 Nisbet, *Émile Durkheim*, p. 50.
20 *Ibid.*, p. 5.
21 *Ibid.*, p. 40.
22 *Ibid.*, p. 58.

, the group from whose nature they spring, before they affect
il as such and establish in him in a new form a purely inner

Such a notion of a society is indeed an abstraction of reality, but it is precisely the kind of abstraction that is necessary to provide a conceptual framework for social planning.

A DEFINITION OF SOCIAL CHANGE

One of the problems in the analysis of social-structural change is the determination of what constitutes change. To resolve this problem requires some recognition of the larger issue of social change.

Social change as system change   By social change we mean some alteration in a social system. The question immediately arises, how much alteration constitutes change: partial modifications or cataclysmic revolutions?

The problem of defining system change in any total sense has been identified by Ernest Nagel.

But the notion of a complete change in the structural form of a society is similarly incoherent. For although one kind of social relationship in "the sum total of all the social relationships" may be totally modified, some other kind of relationship must remain unaltered, albeit this latter kind may happen to be one that is of no interest to us normally. In short, a social system can be said to change its structural form also only in the relative sense of an alteration in some particular kinds of social relationships.[24]

In order to achieve the objectives of change some aspect of the system must remain unchanged or else those original objectives will no longer be relevant.

A general approach to resolving this problem is provided by Lewis A. Coser in his attempt to distinguish changes *of* systems from changes *within* systems.

We propose to talk of a change of system when all major structural relations, its basic institutions, and its prevailing value system have been drastically altered. (In cases where such a change takes place abruptly, as,

23 Émile Durkheim, *Suicide*, trans, John A. Spaulding and George Simpson (New York: The Free Press, 1951), p. 320.

24 Ernest Nagel, *The Structure of Science* (New York: Harcourt, Brace & World Inc., 1961), p. 529.

*for example, the Russian revolution, there should be no difficulty. It is well
to remember, however, that transformations of social systems do not always
consist in an abrupt and simultaneous change of all basic institutions. Institutions may change gradually, by mutual adjustment, and it is only over a
period of time that the observer will be able to claim that the social system
has undergone a basic transformation in its structural relations.) In concrete
historical reality, no clear cut distinctions exist. Change of systems may be
the result (or the sum total) of previous changes within the system. This
does not, however, detract from the usefulness of the theoretical distinction.*[25]

Recognizing the distinction as an abstraction, Coser does provide
two criteria by which to judge system change: (1) the speed or the
time over which change takes place, and (2) the extent of the system
affected by the given change.

Francesca Cancian provides a more specific resolution to this dilemma
of ambiguity.[26] Following Nagel's formulation of the nature of a functional system, Cancian notes that there are two types of variables in
such a system: a *state*, G, a property of the system which is maintained;
and *state coordinates*, factors or forces in the system which determine
the presence of state G. The particular values of the state coordinates
may vary from time to time. However, as long as such variations balance
each other, they produce the net effect of maintaining the state, G. In
such a case they can be said to work in a compensatory manner; any
increase in one state coordinate is compensated for by a decrease in
another state coordinate. Equilibrium is a condition of the system under
which a given state, G, is maintained. The state coordinates are said to
be functional for this state, G.

For example, let G refer to a stable government in a given city, and
let corruption in that form of government be a state coordinate. To the
extent to which corruption serves to maintain the present party in power,
it may be thought of as functional for the state of the system, stable
government. For that party to remain in power, any reduction in corruption would require compensatory action in some other means of
achieving voter support.

Cancian uses this model to distinguish between changes within a
system and changes of a system.

*Change within the system refers to change that does not alter the system's
basic structure. In a functional system, this means changes in state coordi-*

25 Lewis A. Coser, *Continuities in the Study of Social Conflict* (New York: The Free Press,
1967), p. 28.
26 Francesca Cancian, "Functional Analysis of Change," in *Social Change*, eds. Amitai Etzioni
and Eva Etzioni (New York: Basic Books, Inc., Publishers, 1964), pp. 112–25.

nates for which compensation is possible. G and the relationship between state coordinates remain the same. Change of the system is any change that alters the system's basic structure. In a functional system, this includes disappearance of G, the appearance of new state coordinates or the disappearance of old ones, and change in the range of variation of state coordinates for which compensation is possible.[27]

In terms of the model of analysis set forth in this book, a given social problem can be thought of as a particular state of a social system. The social structure of that system can be thought of as a state coordinate which functions to maintain the state G, a social problem. The objective is to identify changes in the social structure that will result in the disappearance of a given state, a social problem. In this sense our analysis deals with changes *of* systems.

But as Cancian points out, systems have subsystems when the total community or the larger society is taken as the frame of reference. As such, subsystems can be treated as state coordinates maintaining a state, G, in a more inclusive system.

Systems can be treated as subsystems, that is as state coordinates maintaining a G in a more inclusive system. Compensating changes in subsystems can be predicted as the result of an "initial" variation in other subsystems that threaten the maintenance of G. In this case, change of a subsystem is change within a more inclusive system.[28]

This distinction between subsystems and inclusive systems is particularly useful for delimiting the meaning of social change as it is treated in this analysis. It makes possible the analysis of change of a particular subsystem which may or may not result in change of a more inclusive system.

The practical focus of this book is on the kinds of social problems faced by such practitioners as social workers, city planners, and public health officers. The scale of social interaction to be analyzed must be commensurate with their scope of operations. The kinds of systems in which they have professional influence are fairly small in relation to the total society. Therefore, the systems of social relationships analyzed in the following chapters involve geographical areas no larger than neighborhoods and population groups contained within the local community. The changes sought are in relation to some state of those small systems, and not necessarily changes in the national society of which these systems are a part.

27 *Ibid.*, p. 119.
28 *Ibid.*, pp. 119f.

Within the context of national society, it is more appropriate to consider the nature of social change with which this book deals as change *of* subsystems. Where these changes can be accomodated by the larger community or national society by compensatory changes in other subsystems, the result is change *within* the national society as an inclusive social system. Where these subsystem changes are not compensatory, the results may well be change *of* the more inclusive social system.

In utilizing this resolution of the dilemma for defining the dimensions of system change, a word of caution is provided by Peter M. Blau.[29] In referring to the distinction alluded to by Cancian, Blau uses the terms "macrostructures" and "microstructures." However, as Blau points out, the constituent elements of systems with such diverse dimensions are different. Microstructures have as their constituent elements interacting individuals or actors in the Parsonian sense. In the case of macrostructures, the constituent elements are other social structures, that is, a macrostructure is, by definition, a complex social structure.

While there are parallels between the social processes in these two different dimensional systems, there are significant differences. The problem of value consensus is critical in macrostructures, whereas in microstructures feelings of personal attraction are sufficient to provide cohesion. In a macrostructure there is interaction between what goes on within the constituent structures and what goes on among structures. And finally macrostructures tend to have enduring institutions whereas microstructures are more transitory. Therefore it should not be assumed that a model of social-structural change of subsystems or microstructures is directly applicable without modification to social-structural change of inclusive systems, or macrosystems.

There is one dissenting comment to be made about this resolution of the dilemma. Cancian leaves one with the impression that there are only two discrete alternatives: (1) changes within the system in which a given state is maintained, and (2) changes of the system in which a given state disappears. It is in this regard that Coser's time perspective becomes relevant. It is difficult to conceive of a situation in which compensatory changes among state coordinates result in maintaining a state G in a precisely consistent condition. Some alterations are bound to occur. Minor, though not necessarily insignificant, changes in system states are often referred to as incremental changes. When such changes are cumulative over time, as Coser points out, they eventually result in basic change of the system.

A classic example of such a phenomenon is the change that has occurred in the American economy over the period 1930 to 1960. The

---

29 Peter M. Blau, "The Structure of Social Associations" in *Sociological Theory*, ed. Walter L. Wallace (Chicago: Aldine Publishing Company, 1969), pp. 187–200.

New Deal legislation of the 1930s can be thought of as attempts to maintain a state G, private control of the economic system, by changing state coordinates, such as the distribution of income between rich and poor. The progressive income tax was a change *of* a subsystem but a change *within* the more inclusive system of the economy as a whole. However these and other subsystem changes have accumulated over time to reduce the role of discretionary capital in the control of individual businesses. By 1960, the American economy was no longer one which was based principally on private entrepreneurship.[30]

Social change as structural change   More specific to the focus of this book is the question of social change as structural change. Such must involve a change in the combination of roles and statuses, and their distribution within a social system.

It can be demonstrated that there are three distinct ways in which such change can occur: (1) by reallocating the existing combination of roles and statuses to a different set of individuals or membership; (2) by altering the combination of roles characteristic of a given structure; or (3) by redistributing the rights and obligations inherent in the statuses of that structure.

These methods are deduced from Parson's discussion of the maintenance of stability in social systems. Parsons observes that one of the important mechanisms for maintaining stability in social structures is the allocation of personnel to roles within that structure.

> There must from the point of view of the going social system, therefore, be a continual process of "replacement" for personnel in the roles of the social system. It is, of course, essential to stability in most cases that this should not come all at once, and it seldom does but nevertheless it is always going on.[31]

Parsons inadvertently suggests how this process of replacement may result in structural change. When the replacement of personnel in the roles of the social structure occurs all at once, or in large doses, significant changes in role definition or performance can result. Parsons observes, in fact, that one of the characteristics of a new social structure is the coincidence between the initial allocation of roles to individuals and the entrance of actors into the role system.

Parsons does not explain why replacement results in changes in role definition or enactment. Presumably such changes stem from different

---

30 For an elaboration of this observation, see Galbraith, *The New Industrial State.*
31 Parsons, *The Social System,* p. 117.

sets of values, interests, or goals held by the new complement of actors. A vivid example of such a process is the more aggressive role of students following the introduction of significant numbers of non-middle class black students into college systems.

The second method of structural change has to do with innovations in roles. Parsons recognizes that the role structure of a system is never completely fixed.

> *Most social systems are dynamically changing in this as in other respects. But room for change does not mean that any actor or group of them can "innovate" by redefining their roles in any way they may happen to desire. Some types of such innovation are compatible to the stability of the social system while others are not. Hence the institutionalization of patterns of legitimation of private role innovation is one important context of regulation of permissiveness.[32]*

Thus, given a group of actors in a social system, it is possible to change the structure by creating new roles or redefining existing roles. Linton recognizes the same process in noting that role patterns may be changed as a result of the introduction of a new type of social relationship.

> *If a new social situation develops, say the introduction of the employer-employee relationship into a society which previously lacked anything of the sort, the behavior between individuals standing in the new relationship will at first be unpatterned. . . . In time those standing in the new relationship will develop forms of behavior which are simultaneously effective in the new relationship and compatible with the pre-existing patterns.[33]*

Conversely, the set of roles which constitute a given structure may be altered by obsolescence. This process has been particularly evident with regard to the role of elderly people in our society. In fact, the central crisis facing the elderly has been the marked reduction in their traditional roles resulting from technological changes in the larger society over the last fifty years.

And finally, the third method of structural change is suggested by Parsons' reference to the allocation of rewards within a structure.

> *The second context is regulation of the processes of allocation of personnel where the problem is to see that the "right" people get into the right roles, and that people stay "where they belong" in terms of status. Essentially the same is to be said about the regulation of the allocation of facilities of*

32 *Ibid.*, p. 133.
33 Linton, *The Study of Man*, p. 106.

rewards, heading as they do up to the political power problem and the prestige problem.[34]

Thus by a redistribution of the rewards and obligations inherent in various statuses, the relative attractiveness of certain positions can change resulting in their redistribution among the actors in a social system. The most notable example of this process has been the change in the occupational structure of our labor market. Whereas years ago unskilled and service occupations, particularly those involved in agriculture, drew large numbers of workers into their ranks, today they are a small part of the total labor force. The advent of increased technology has resulted in giving more weight to technical occupations than to labor-intensive occupations.

Although the most obvious way in which such redistribution takes place is as the result of technological innovations, there is another source of redistribution that is particularly relevant to the cases chosen for analysis in this book. In his discussion of exchange processes governing social interaction, Blau notes that unequal distribution of power, or shifts in the balance of power among actors, can result in a sense of disadvantage, and can precipitate social movements that attempt to right this imbalance of power.[35] This process is also referred to by Parsons in his discussion of revolutionary movements as a source of social change.[36]

In considering the distribution of obligations as an aspect of social structures, an interesting analysis of change is provided, again by Parsons.[37] A change in the distribution of obligations can come about through the formation of deviant subcultures or contracultures within any given system. As members of a system who have become alienated—by crime, mental illness, or other forms of deviancy—achieve a group identity out of a common sense of alienation, they develop a sense of solidarity. This solidarity makes possible a deviant subculture such as skid row or the "hippie" communes. Such groups serve to reinforce the deviancy of their members and to protect them against the sanctions of the larger social system. Hence, their former obligation to behave in certain ways is altered, resulting in a changed social structure with respect to their system of interaction.

In summary then we would expect social-structural change to occur under any of the following three conditions: (1) when the group of

---

34 Parsons, *The Social System*, pp. 133f.
35 Peter M. Blau, "The Structure of Social Associations," *op. cit.*, p. 1.
36 Talcott Parsons, *The Social System*, Chapter 11.
37 *Ibid.*

actors among whom the basic roles and statuses are allocated is significantly changed, (2) when there is a change in the combinations of roles through obsolescence or an introduction of new roles into a social system, or (3) when there is a redistribution of rewards and obligations among the various statuses within the social structure. /

Exogenous and endogenous sources of change   In the traditional literature dealing with social systems, there has been a tendency to analyze change in terms of sources within the system itself, called *endogenous* factors, rather than sources external to the system, called *exogenous* factors.

In a recent analysis of social change from an historical point of view, Nisbet has drawn attention to the limitations of such an understanding.[38] More often than not, changes in social systems or social structures result from invasion from the outside, that is contact with other systems. Technological innovation is the most potent of such factors. In contrast, functionalism tends to explain change by reference to endogenous factors such as role differentiation and strains. Endogenous factors may be appropriate for explaining why systems persist, but they are not very adequate for explaining why they change. As Nisbet points out, functionalism is a good theory of stability but a bad theory of change.

Above all, we shall not find the sources of change in society through efforts which seek to deduce it as a fixed property of social structures. Change can no more be deduced from social structure and its processes than these latter can be deduced from the elements of human psychology.[39]

The approach to social-structural change that characterizes this book is consistent with Nisbet's caution. The origin of structural change is not posited in terms of internal factors within systems of social relationships. On the contrary, ways are sought by which the planners, usually from some point outside the system, can act on the system or subsystem to bring about structural change. The source of such change is not specified in advance, the only constraint is that structural change be the factor that accounts for the change in a state of a given social system.[40]

---

38 Robert A. Nisbet, *Social Change and History* (New York: Oxford University Press, Inc., 1969).

39 *Ibid.*, p. 303.

40 This view of social change as a result of factors impinging on systems as well as from within systems is consistent with the view of Duncan and Schnore. They prefer an ecological context within which to view social change, which places social organization in an environmental context and thus incorporates technological as well as social factors in the social change process. See Otis Dudley Duncan and Leo F. Schnore, "Cultural, Behavioral and Ecological Perspectives in the Study of Social Organization," *Sociological Theory*, ed. Walter L. Wallace (Chicago: Aldine Publishing Company, 1969), pp. 70–88.

Structural change and residual treatment   Implicit in the assumptions that underlie this treatment of the subject is a contrast between two alternative means of social intervention. The one, called residual treatment, is focused on altering the individual exhibiting the problematic behavior in such a way as to relieve the sources of the problem in the individual or to improve his position relative to other individuals within the system. The second, identified as structural change, focuses on altering the system of social relationships in which problematic behavior occurs.[41]

The first approach, of course, is based on a model of individual treatment that has been traditional in the field of social welfare and among the "helping professions." It rests on the assumption that the origins of the problem lie in some form of pathology in the individual or in the way he relates to his social environment. It is called residual because it does not attack the system as a whole but simply those elements or individuals within the system who do not benefit from it, whose problems are a by-product of an otherwise adequately functioning system.

The second approach rests on a model of social change. It posits the source of the problem in the social arrangements which exist between those who exhibit the problematic behavior and the "significant others" with whom they interact. Changes in these arrangements affect everyone in the system of relationships regardless of his individual preferences. As a result, these two alternative models of intervention have different consequences, both for the problem and for the social group within which the problem takes place.

Structural change is more likely to be preventative because it attacks those factors in the situation that precipitate or aggravate problematic behavior. In contrast, residual treatments, to the extent that causation stems from the social structure, are constantly employed against a never ending flow of casualties.

Structural change is more pervasive in the sense that it affects all individuals in the system, not just those exhibiting the problematic behavior. In contrast, residual treatment is more selective; it affects only those individuals treated or who are willing to be treated. In this lies the strength and weakness of structural change: it does not depend on self selection as does residual treatment, but at the same time it generates more resistance, more social conflict, because individuals must take some action to avoid being affected.

---

41 This contrast in strategies and its implications for the inclusive system is amplified in Arthur Blum, *et al.*, "Goals and Means for Social Change," in *Neighborhood Organization for Community Action*, ed. John B. Turner (New York: National Association of Social Workers, 1968), pp. 106–32.

And thirdly, structural change is likely to be less profound in terms of its effect on any one individual. It corrects only those deficiencies that can be traced to the social structure of the situation, and leaves untouched those factors that may derive from individual biological or psychological systems. Residual treatment, on the other hand, can attempt to treat all effects in an individual case through some kind of action, be it to insulate, rehabilitate, or palliate.

In the analysis of cases in this book, these two points of view will be contrasted as a means of clarifying the distinctive nature of social-structural change. However, as is evident from the above discussion, there is no assumption that social-structural change is always preferable to residual treatment. Rather, social-structural change is presented in a manner to elaborate its full potential as an alternative to the models of intervention that presently dominate practice theories.

Chapter 3

CASE STUDIES IN
SOCIAL-STRUCTURAL CHANGE:
CHANGING THE MEMBERSHIP

INTRODUCTION

The major interest of this book lies in the elaboration of social structural change as a method of solving social problems. The term social structure, as used in the field of sociology, has come to mean the arrangement among persons or actors in a system of social relationships based on their status and role.

As pointed out in Chapter 2, there appear to be three ways of changing social structures. One is to change the type of personnel or the set of individuals who occupy the structure. This will be referred to as changing the membership of the social structure. Another involves changing the roles or role combinations that constitute the structure. The third involves changing the statuses of members of the structure by redistributing rights and obligations inherent in those statuses.

In the present chapter, we will analyze cases involving changes in the membership of social structures. Chapter 4 will be devoted to case studies which involve changing the set of roles of a given structure. In

Chapter 5 we will examine cases in which structural change consisted of a redistribution of rights and obligations inherent in statuses.

Before proceeding with these analyses, it will be helpful to review the method to be used in relation to the purposes to be achieved.

METHOD OF ANALYSIS

Object of analysis   As stated in Chapter 1, the purpose of this volume is to find answers to two questions: (1) how are social problems translated into social-structural terms, and (2) what tools are available to the planner for structural intervention?

With respect to the first objective, interest lies in the way problems are conceptualized rather than the validity of the underlying theoretical assumptions. Similarly, in examining solutions to problems, interest lies in the identification of opportunities for structural intervention rather than the efficacy of the proposed solutions.

Logical rather than empirical validity is the primary issue in the analysis of cases. Of course, the implications generated by this analysis must not be refutable by established theory nor fly in the face of empirical evidence. The primary test of adequacy is whether or not the change identified deals with social structure, and whether or not the method of achieving change involves techniques or resources available to a policy-making body within the context of the local community.

Operationalizing social-structural change   In operational terms, social-structural change reduces to two basic processes: (1) incorporating different people into the same structure, or (2) incorporating the same people into different structures. Thus, the operational definition of social-structural change implies simply an alteration in the composition of either the actors in the structure or the roles and/or statuses of the structure.

The principal problem in utilizing this definition involves the ability to separate structural effects from individual effects.

Social structure is a theoretical construct. It has no direct empirical referent. Its existence can be inferred only from simpler concepts of which it consists. For example, the effects of the class structure can be observed only in terms of the effects of occupation and education of which it consists. However, occupation and education are characteristics of individuals as well as of structures. In measuring change in the composition of the membership of a social structure, therefore, we must ask ourselves whether differences in the resulting behavior arise from changes in the structure of the group, or merely from a different accumulation of individuals being observed. Similarly, when the roles of a particular social structure are augmented, is the difference in observed behavior a result of a change in the nature of all roles, or simply a reflection of the added behavior emanating from the new roles?

The task of devising a method of distinguishing structural effects from individual effects has already been accomplished by James A. Davis and others in what has been called "compositional" or "contextual" analysis.[1] Compositional analysis is a technique for isolating in a measurable way the effect of a characteristic of a group with respect to a given independent variable, in contrast to the effect of the possession of that attribute by an individual. Thus, for example, a Democrat in a town composed predominantly of Democrats may exhibit different political behavior from a Democrat in a town with a Republican majority. To constitute a compositional effect, the characteristic of the group must be shown to affect individuals who do not share that attribute, or to accentuate the effect of the characteristic on those who do.

Social compositional analysis is accomplished in the following manner. A group characteristic (Durkheim's social fact) is selected as an independent variable. Its counterpart in terms of individual attributes is determined. A change in the behavior of individuals composing the group is specified as the dependent variable. While varying the composition of the group in terms of the independent variable, and controlling for the presence of this characteristic among individuals within the group, the variations in the dependent variable are measured.

With reference to the example of the voting behavior of Democrats, party affiliation would be the independent variable, and voting behavior would be the dependent variable. Towns with varying proportions of registered Democrats would be selected. The voting patterns of registered Democrats within those towns would be observed. Assuming the usual controls for spurious influences, the differences in the proportion of Democrats voting Democratic would be a reflection of the effect of the social structure of the respective communities.

A crucial step in this procedure is conceptualizing the independent variable. It must represent an empirical referent of some aspect of social structure in order to provide the basis for inferences regarding the effects of structural change.

1 James A. Davis, Joe L. Spaeth, and Caroline Huson, "A Technique for Analyzing the Effects of Group Composition," *American Sociological Review*, 26 (April 1961), 215–26; and Peter M. Blau, "Formal Organization: Dimensions of Analysis," *American Journal of Sociology*, 63 (July 1957), 58–69.

Davis identifies a variety of compositional effects. Awareness of these variations will be helpful in pursuing the analyses undertaken in this book. For example, in some cases a variation in the group composition may be accompanied by no variation in individual behavior with respect to the dependent variable. In such a case, social-structural change can be said to have no influence (see Figure I, Graph A). The opposite extreme is represented by the case in which all individuals, regardless of their differences with respect to the independent variable, respond identically in relation to changes in the group composition. Such a case is useful for explaining the process, but is not likely to occur in real life. This effect would be graphed by a single inclined line (Figure I, Graph B).

In between these two extremes are several alternative patterns of compositional effect that are more likely to reflect actual experience. One is the case in which structural change affects both high and low individuals in a similar direction, but in which the individual differences persist (Figure I, Graph C). A second alternative is one in which variations in the group composition are accompanied by differential changes in various types of individuals within the group, some responding positively and others negatively. Such an effect can be graphed by intersecting lines (Figure I, Graph D). Another variation of this same pattern is the case in which individuals with one set of values on the independent variable are affected by changes in group composition while individuals with another set of values remain unchanged creating a converging or diverging pattern (Figure I, Graph E). The last alternative reflects a curvilinear relationship between changes in the group composition and individual behavior. In other words, the effect of group composition varies at different levels of structural change, resulting in a graph with a series of plateaus and slopes (Figure I, Graph F). Such graphs can be very useful for identifying critical points for policy change.

While Davis's method implies alterations in the membership of groups, there seems to be no reason why the method could not be extended to alterations in structural phenomena as defined in this volume.

For example, it should be possible to measure the effect of variations in statuses on individual behavior. In fact, as much is implied in Davis's treatment of the theory of relative deprivation.[2] In this analysis, Davis differentiates individuals on the basis of some characteristic of desirability, the absence of which creates in the individual a sense of depriva-

---

2 James A. Davis, "A Formal Interpretation of the Theory of Relative Deprivation," *Sociometry*, **22** (December 1959), 280–96.

FIGURE 1:
Graphs of alternative effects of group compositional change.

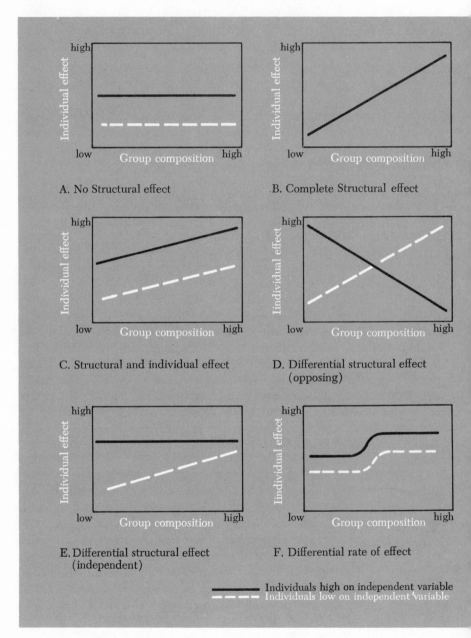

A. No Structural effect

B. Complete Structural effect

C. Structural and individual effect

D. Differential structural effect (opposing)

E. Differential structural effect (independent)

F. Differential rate of effect

————— Individuals high on independent variable
– – – – – Individuals low on independent variable

tion. This in essence reflects hierarchical status. He observes:

> When a deprived person compares himself with a non-deprived, the result-
> ing state will be called "relative deprivation." When a non-deprived person
> compares himself with a deprived person, the resulting state will be called
> "relative gratification."[3]

The amount of relative deprivation or gratification, therefore, is a function of the group's composition with respect to some state of desirability. If many are in an undesirable state the amount of relative deprivation will be small, if very few are in an undesirable state the amount of relative deprivation will be high.

A similar extension of the notion of compositional analysis can be made with respect to the role structure of a social group. The "maximum feasible participation" of the poor in the War on Poverty is an example of a change in role composition. In social agencies, the traditional structure consisting of two roles, those of the client and the clinician, has been augmented by the role of the resident or neighborhood-aide who functions as an intermediary. This change in the composition of roles has affected the behavior of both the clients and the clinicians.

In summary then, social-structural change is reflected in alterations in the composition of a social group in terms of its membership, its statuses or positions of desirability, or its roles, while holding constant the comparable characteristics of individuals in that group.

Variables to be analyzed   The objectives set forth at the outset of this book lead to the selection of three basic variables for analysis: (1) social problems, (2) structural phenomena, and (3) tools of intervention. Since this strategy is more complex than the two-variable model used in compositional analysis, some explanation is needed.

Social problems, as we use that term consist of conditions or behavior of individuals which in some way arouse a degree of public concern. Typical examples are poverty, crime, illness, discrimination, poor housing, and acts of violence. Such *social problems constitute the dependent variable* in this analysis.

Structural phenomena consist of aspects of social structure, i.e., actors, roles, and statuses. However, because our objective is to push the analysis of change back to the role of the planner, *structural phenomena constitute an intervening variable.*

3 *Ibid.*, p. 283.

Tools of intervention represent actions promulgated by the planner. They refer to controls over the system of social relationships which can be exercised to change structural phenomena. In this analysis, *tools of intervention constitute the independent variable.*

Criteria for the selection of cases   Social-structural change as a method of problem solving is applicable to social groups of any size, from small friendship clubs to national societies. However, since the needs that motivate the writing of this book are rooted in problems facing urban planners, our analysis focuses on the level of social systems represented by the urban community or its major parts. For this reason, cases were selected which deal with social problems and systems of social relationships prevalent in urban communities.

In addition to the geographical dimension of social systems, the selection of cases was guided by a desire to reflect variation in the three basic variables under consideration. In terms of social problems, the cases represent the range of issues in urban policy confronting planners irrespective of their professional discipline. In terms of social structure, the cases present problems that are conceptualized according to different aspects of social structure, the arrangement of individuals by status and role, or the membership of the system of social relationships. In terms of intervention tools, the cases represent structural phenomena that are amenable to manipulation by a variety of devices.

DEUTSCH AND COLLINS: INTERRACIAL HOUSING

Social problem   The first three cases deal with a social problem by changing the membership composition of social groups involved.

The first case is the landmark study of interracial housing undertaken by Deutsch and Collins.[4] The social problem with which Deutsch and Collins deal is racial prejudice. Conducted during the 1940s, their problem focus was slightly different from today's concern with racism. Nevertheless, the study is relevant to a serious social problem facing urban planners: the relationship between subgroups of the community based on prejudice. Racial prejudice is significant because it can result in violent behavior between groups, and can prevent the expenditure of limited resources for the attainment of more useful objectives. In addi-

4 Morton Deutsch and Mary Evans Collins, "Interracial Housing," in *American Social Patterns,* ed. William Peterson (Garden City, N.Y.: Doubleday & Company, Inc., 1965), pp. 7–62.

tion, prejudice held by those in control of resources can result in discrimination in their distribution against other groups not in power.

Conceptualization of the problem   Deutsch and Collins perceive prejudice as fostered in the segregated pattern of urban neighborhoods.

Thus one result of residential segregation is that prejudiced whites have little opportunity to see Negroes in social contexts which bring out the fundamental condition humaine *of Negroes and whites. They do not see the Negroes, for example, as school children disliking homework, as expectant mothers in their first pregnancy, as tenants complaining about their landlords, or as bread winners facing a contracting labor market.*[5]

Deutsch and Collins argued from what has come to be known as the equal status contact theory of prejudice reduction. Physical proximity encourages social contact. When those contacts are between persons of different subgroups but equal social status, persons in one subgroup who have prejudices against members of the other group will experience a reduction in such prejudice.

In order to test this hypothesis, the authors studied four public housing projects with varying proportions of Negro occupancy. Two were in New York City which had an official policy of integration, that is, families were assigned to buildings without regard to race. In project I, Negroes constituted 70 percent of tenants, and in project II they constituted 40 percent. The other two projects were in the city of Newark, which had an official policy of segregation, in other words families were assigned to different buildings within the project, according to race. Newark project I was 66 percent black, project II 50 percent black. In addition, buildings were clustered according to their racial assignment, further isolating white families from black families.

Since the study was *ex post facto* in design, the problem of controlling for alternative influences on attitude change was critical. This the authors handled with laudable skill. Certain factors were controlled by the nature of the housing market. For example, social class was effectively held constant because both projects were restricted to families with extremely low income. Self selection by occupants on the basis of their predisposition to racial prejudice was controlled in a variety of indirect ways. In the first place the projects were occupied during a period of extreme housing shortage, in essence restricting alternative options for low income families. This shortage would tend to mitigate

5 *Ibid.,* pp. 8f.

persons' refusing residency because of the occupancy pattern of a given project. As a check on this assumption, the authors examined the rate of refusal in the New York projects, which were integrated, and found it to be extremely low, 5 percent for all reasons. Voluntary move-outs were infrequent.

Furthermore all projects were located in predominantly Negro neighborhoods. If voluntary choice in applying for housing were operating, it would have had more of a deterring effect in Newark, than in New York. In the case of Newark, white families choosing a segregated project would be choosing to live in a predominantly black neighborhood. The fact that all other public housing projects in the city of Newark were predominantly white, makes such a process highly unlikely. The authors conclude that social class and self-selection were effectively eliminated as a basis for explaining the results from these different housing patterns.

However there are other important factors which could account for differences in response to housing patterns. The authors were able to control for predispositions towards racial tolerance such as religion, education, political ideology, and previous contact with Negroes, by gathering data on such characteristics in interviews with occupants. Although there was a large difference between the integrated projects in New York and the segregated projects in Newark with respect to the proportion of families who were Jewish, as well as the proportion of families who were liberal in political ideology, these differences when controlled did not eliminate the differences between projects in the degree of contact with Negro neighbors (See Table I).

The results of the Deutsch and Collins study show that integrated projects had a positive impact on relations between the races, and on the attitudes of white women toward their black neighbors. White women in the integrated projects were more likely to have contact with Negro women, to have Negro friends, and to engage in neighborhood activities with Negroes than were white women in the segregated projects.[6] In addition, women in the integrated projects were more likely to express positive attitudes toward Negroes, and on the basis of recall were more likely to report a positive change in attitude since living in the project. It is interesting to note that the positive changes in attitudes and experience were greater in the New York I project with a 70 percent Negro occupancy than in the New York II project with only 40 percent Negro occupancy. This finding, though small, suggests that the change is linear, and is contrary to the "tipping point" theory of interracial relationships.

6 This research was done prior to the widespread adoption of tests of statistical significance in social research. However, the differences between integrated projects and segregated projects are of such size that their statistical significance is virtually assured.

TABLE 1   *Selected responses of white housewives in integrated versus segregated housing*

Selected Responses	Integrated Projects		Segregated Projects	
	New York I (Negroes = 70%) (N=90)	New York II (Negroes = 40%) (N=102)	Newark I (Negroes = 66%) (N=100)	Newark II (Negroes = 50%) (N=101)
Had no neighborly relations with Negroes	28%	61%	99%	96%
Liberal	36%	60%	100%	92%
Jewish	13%	67%	100%	95%
Characteristics attributed to Negroes				
Positive	83%	73%	46%	48%
Negative	32%	39%	54%	47%
Original attitude toward Negroes unfavorable, present attitude favorable	55%	50%	8%	8%
Original attitude neutral, present attitude favorable	69%	50%	24%	13%

SOURCE: Morton Deutsch and Mary Evans Collins, "Interracial Housing," in American Social Patterns, ed. William Peterson (Garden City, N.Y.: Doubleday & Company, Inc., 1965), Tables 1, 2, 4.

Social structure   Deutsch and Collins conceptualize the problem of racial prejudice within the context of the system of social relationships found among neighbors. The structural feature of this system which they chose to treat as their intervening variable is membership composition based on race. They explicitly hold role and status constant. This is a case of putting different actors into the same structure.

Treating the physically proximate neighbors of the white families as the social group, Deutsch and Collins show essentially three variations in racial composition. One in which there are virtually no Negroes (represented by the whites living in segregated projects), a second one in which there are approximately 40 percent Negroes (New York I) and a third in which Negroes constitute 70 percent of the neighboring group (New York II).

However, it is not possible to grasp the compositional effect of such change on the basis of the Deutsch and Collins study alone; they provide data on only one side of the interaction, namely white. To complete the picture it is necessary to know the effects of such compositional change on the black families involved.

Such data are available from a replication study conducted by Ernest Works using the same hypotheses, a similar setting, and Negro interviewers.[7]

Using a housing project in which Negroes constituted 54 percent of the occupants, and one in which they occupied 94 percent of the units, the Works study is comparable in composition to the Newark and New York II projects. However, the effects were more pronounced. Three percent of the Negro women in the integrated project had no contact with the white neighbors, while 27 percent had none in the segregated project. This finding indicates that for Negroes there is a greater likelihood of interracial contact than for white women regardless of the segregated situation. Similarly with respect to attitudes toward their white neighbors, 91 percent in the integrated project had positive attitudes while 44 percent had positive attitudes in the segregated project. Again assuming comparability of data, this finding would suggest that the blacks were more favorably disposed toward outgroup members than was true of whites regardless of the composition.

On the basis of these two studies, it is possible to graph the effects of interracial equal status contacts on both whites and blacks. Since only three variations in composition are available for whites and only two for blacks, the slope of the respective curves can only be estimated. It appears that the curve for the black housewives is consistently higher than the curve for the white housewives, that they are essentially parallel, and that both incline with an increasing proportion of Negroes among neighbors, as illustrated in Figure 2.

Tool of intervention   The point of intervention into this system of social relationships to which the urban planner has access are the policies governing the management of public housing. In this particular case, the point of intervention is quite clear: public housing authorities have governing bodies established by law whose actions are accessible to public scrutiny. The policies of such bodies determine the eligibility requirements for residence in such projects and thus they can monitor changes in the composition over time.

While it would be naïve to assume that such governing boards are necessarily responsive to planners' recommendations, or that policies are

7 Ernest Works, "The Prejudice-interaction Hypothesis from the Point of View of the Negro Minority Group," *The American Journal of Sociology*, 67 (July 1961), 47–53.

FIGURE 2:
Effect of change in racial composition on attitudes
toward opposite race.

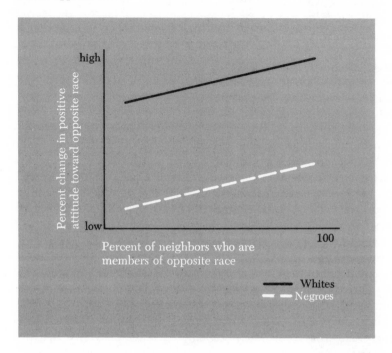

readily manipulatable, such a point of intervention is accessible to a
planner. The methods he must use to achieve policy changes are the
subject of another study reported earlier.[8]

Residual alternatives   How does such an approach differ from the
alternative of an individual treatment model of change?

A contrasting approach would focus on individual persons who exhibit
prejudice and attempt to change their prejudicial attitudes. Such efforts
are more typical of the educational programs of organizations concerned
with intergroup relations. While from a structural point of view such
programs may be essential for reinforcing society's norms of tolerance
and acceptance of group differences, and for supporting public policies
of integration, they do not constitute intervention at the level of social
interaction.

8 See Morris and Binstock, *Feasible Planning for Social Change.*

Implications for social policy   Because of the current public interest in integration, or desegregation as it is more accurately called, as a public policy with regard to education, it is important to take note of the implications of the Deutsch and Collins findings for this larger policy issue. It is very tempting to project the findings of a clear, uncomplicated, and well-documented study as a solution to all situations of that general class. Since any study, no matter how throughly executed, is an oversimplification of reality, such a practice is likely to be disappointing. To argue that the physical mixing of races in all situations will result in prejudice reduction is absurd.

In a replication study by Wilner, Walkley, and Cook, the central conditions under which the Deutsch and Collins hypothesis hold true are set forth.[9] They are: (1) the members of the different racial groups between whom contact takes place must be of equal social status, (2) the circumstances of such contact must not be marked by competition for limited goods, and (3) the contact must take place in an atmosphere not marked by strong social disapproval of intergroup friendliness.

Such conditions raise serious questions about the possibility of achieving positive attitude change from school desegregation. For example, Deutsch and Collins themselves argue that housing integration would not bring positive results in the South where community attitudes may be hostile toward interracial mixing. Furthermore, when school desegregation mixes lower class children of one race with middle class children of another race, the results may actually increase or verify negative stereotypes rather than disprove them. And lastly, a school situation is very different from a housing project; the school is marked by competition for scarce resources in the form of grades or rank in class. Such circumstances may harden racial attitudes rather than obliterate them. A housing project is not marked by such circumstances.

Awareness of the more precise applicability of the findings of the Deutsch and Collins study can lead to more effective public policy. This awareness increases our understanding of the argument of the black separatists who point out that desegregation in the absence of mutual respect results in assimilation at best and subjugation at worst.

ROSOW: SOCIAL INTEGRATION OF THE AGED

Social problem   A problem of widespread concern is the social isolation of elderly persons. The magnitude and the severity of this problem is especially characteristic of older industrial cities in the North and

9 Daniel M. Wilner, Rosabelle Price Walkley, and Stuart W. Cook, *Human Relations in Interracial Housing* (Minneapolis, Minn.: Univ. of Minnesota Press, 1955).

the East. Here persons of retirement age have spent their years of employment in industries with limited or no retirement benefits and minimal coverage under the Social Security Act. In addition, such industries are likely to have paid marginal wages over the lifetime of the retired worker. These economic hardships are complicated by the out-migration of the younger generation to the Mid-west and Far-west where economic opportunity has been greater over the past twenty years, leaving elderly parents essentially isolated from family contact.[10]

The result of these developments can be seen in the clusters of rooming houses and cheap apartments in and around the core of cities inhabited by elderly people on substandard or marginal incomes. The problem facing the urban planner arises not only from the need to provide the necessary services for this dependent segment of the population, but also from the fact that this group frequently requires relocation in the course of rebuilding the central cities.[11]

Conceptualization of the problem   The community has been conceptualized as a social system based on territoriality that functions to meet the basic human needs of its member households. One of these needs is for friendship or relationships of mutual support.[12]

We have abundant literature on the effect of neighborhood on such relationships. One study by Irving Rosow demonstrates clearly the effect of the social composition of the neighborhood on its function of fostering relationships of mutual support among the aged.[13]

Rosow's conceptualization of the problem is based on an extensive review of the literature on friendship formation. One theoretical assumption underlying his work is that friendships are primarily made in the context of peer groups. "Friendship circles consist of people with similar positions, life styles, and beliefs. Insofar as aging represents a major status change, relative age statuses will be central to our problem and our basic research design."[14]

The other assumption is based on the increasing importance of physical proximity for meeting the needs of the elderly. With increasing age, elderly persons, regardless of social class, become increasingly dependent on local friendship ties, those based in the neighborhood. This assumption is based on the fact that with increasing age persons lose

10 David Joyce, Robert R. Mayer, and Mary Nenno, *The Social Functioning of the Dislodged Elderly* (Philadelphia, Pa.: Institute for Environmental Studies, University of Pennsylvania, 1966).

11 Paul L. Niebark, *Relocation in Urban Planning: From Obstacle to Opportunity* (Philadelphia, Pa.: University of Pennsylvania Press, 1968), pp. 29–50.

12 Roland L. Warren, *The Community in America* (Chicago: Rand McNally & Co., 1963), pp. 167–208.

13 Irving Rosow, *Social Integration of the Aged* (New York: The Free Press, 1967).

14 *Ibid.*, p. 27.

other sources of friendship through loss of employment, declining physical health, and death of marriage partners.

Given these assumptions, Rosow makes the following hypotheses:

> *We predict that* the number of their local friends and the amount of their interaction with neighbors will be directly related to the residential concentration of the aged. Furthermore this general relationship will be intensified for those with high role loss, high dependency on the local environment, and normatively lower status positions, particularly of social class, sex, and marital status.[15]

In order to test these hypotheses, 1200 elderly persons living in three different types of residential settings in Cleveland were interviewed. A residential setting was defined as an apartment building.[16] In order for an apartment building to be included in the study 90 percent of its residents had to be in the same occupational class, dichotomized as manual or non-manual. Three classes of such apartment buildings were used for the sample: those with a *normal* proportion of households containing an aged member (1 to 15 percent), those with a *concentrated* elderly population (33 to 49 percent of the households having elderly members), and those with a *dense* population of elderly (50 percent or greater). Social integration was measured by sociometric questions eliciting the number of friends a respondent had among his neighbors[17] and the frequency of contact with such friends in a week.

The findings supported the first hypothesis. Even when the data were controlled for social class, the average number of local friends increased with a greater age concentration in residential settings. For working class elderly living in normal settings, the average number of neighbor-friends was 1.48, while for those in dense settings the average was 2.12. For middle class elderly normal settings produced an average of 1.33 neighbor-friends, while dense settings raised the average to 1.64.

These figures minimize the actual differences between areas of different age composition. In the first place *sociometric data were recorded only on the first three friends mentioned.* Therefore the averages have a maximum range of zero to three. Furthermore, *the persons who mentioned more than three friends were more frequently found in dense apartments.* Consequently the findings with respect to the first hypothesis underestimate the effect of age concentration in residential settings on social integration.

Rosow's analysis of the social integration of the elderly is limited as

---

15 *Ibid.*, p. 41.
16 No further operationalizing of the concept was provided by the author.
17 No further operationalizing of the concept was provided by the author.

an application of the pure model of social-compositional analysis in two ways: (1) It analyzes the differential concentration of age groups in different residential contexts, but it does not analyze the differential age of individuals living in that group; in other words, he does not show what effect age concentration has on the non-elderly. (2) Rosow's data can only indirectly show that residential concentration has an effect beyond the greater numerical availability of persons with whom to interact. By restricting his measure of social integration to neighbor-friends, he cannot show that increased sociability with neighbors is not simply a displacement of friendships which otherwise might have been made outside the neighborhood, leaving the total number of friends unchanged. It would have been preferable to measure the total number of friends irrespective of their location as the dependent variable.

In testing his second hypothesis, Rosow seeks to show the effect of two intervening variables—role loss and social class—on the relationship between the residential setting and social integration. In Figure 3 it can

FIGURE 3:
Effect of role loss and residential concentration of elderly on contact with neighbors—working class respondents.

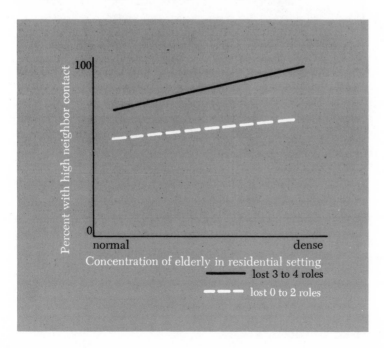

be seen that all working class persons increase their number of neighbor-friends with increased concentration of elderly in the environment; but for those with high role loss, this effect is accentuated.

However, middle class elderly show a different pattern (see Figure 4). Those with low role loss show little effect of residential concentration by age on the number of neighbor-friends they have. Those with high role loss are positively affected by such concentration.

FIGURE 4:

Effect of role loss and residential concentration of elderly on contact with neighbors—middle class respondents.

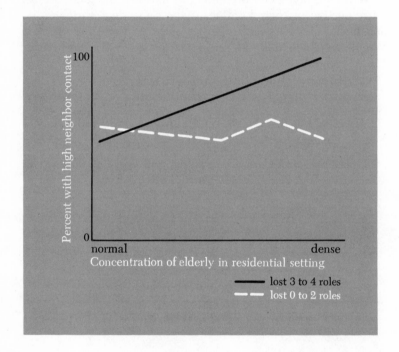

Social structure   The system of social relationships in this case is identical to that of the Deutsch and Collins case, the relationships of friendship and mutual support which exist among neighbors. The structure consists essentially of equal status—neighbors are expected to be friendly, helpful, and egalitarian in their dealings with one another. Similarly, change was formulated in terms of the composition of actors located in that structure, rather than changing the roles or statuses prevailing among neighbors.

Rosow reasoned, on the basis of prior research, that the system of relationships among friends requires a structure of statuses that are essentially equal. Since the aged suffer from lower status in the larger society in several respects, placing them in the position of neighbors with young people would inhibit the development of friendships. Thus, changing the composition of actors permits the structure of relationships among neighbors to be more conducive to social integration.

Tool of intervention   The point of intervention in this system of relationships is likewise similar to the Deutsch and Collins case. To the extent that housing developments are subject to public sanctions either through governmental or voluntary organizations, their composition can be controlled by tenant selection policies.

However, this case suggests some alternative possibilities. There are opportunities for intervention other than the policies of bodies that manage housing units. Control over the private housing market can be exercised through the control of land use for new construction and public expenditures as incentives for housing for the aged. In addition, in the course of relocation due to governmental actions, elderly people can be directed to those environments that are most conducive to their social integration.[18]

Residual alternative   The residual alternatives to housing policies provide a dramatic contrast to structural approaches. Social workers have tended to respond to the increased isolation that accompanies old age by organizing golden age clubs. As Rosow points out, such clubs reach no more than five percent of the elderly population in most American cities.[19] In light of these facts, a much more effective method would appear to be the creation of housing developments in which at least 50 percent of the units are occupied by elderly residents—a method that utilizes the natural process of social integration in the neighborhood.

Implications for social policy   The Rosow study actually grew out of a policy debate in the field of gerontology—whether elderly persons were better off in intergenerational environments or in environments dominated by their own age group. The findings of the study support the latter view. Such a policy will be more crucial for working class than for middle class elderly, and with those in all social classes who have experienced role loss.

18 Joyce, et al., *The Social Functioning of the Dislodged Elderly*, p. 67.
19 *Ibid.*, p. 20.

The findings of the Rosow study should not be construed to imply severance of all contact with the younger generation. The findings indicate that only 50 percent of the immediate neighbors need be elderly to achieve the maximum benefit for social integration. In addition, the housing development is a base for daily social interaction. It enables the elderly to arrange visits with children and family at times and places of their own choosing.

ROSENBERG: ADOLESCENT SELF-IMAGE

Social problem   The third case involving the membership composition of the neighborhood is based on the study by Rosenberg of social influences on self-esteem and psychological disturbance among adolescents.[20] The study deals with the general problem of how to reduce manifestations of mental illness.

The author seeks to explain the prevalence of emotional insecurity during the adolescent years. He notes the increased vulnerability to emotional insecurity among adolescents arising from the absence of a well defined social position for persons who are neither children nor adults. "Late adolescence is a period of unusual status ambiguity. Society does not have a clear set of expectations for the adolescent.[21]

Rosenberg operationalizes his dependent variable in terms of two basic characteristics: (1) low self-esteem and (2) psychosomatic symptoms. "The presence of low self-esteem among neurotics is commonly observed in clinical practice. Indeed, some clinicians go so far as to characterize low self-esteem as one of the basic elements of neurosis."[22]

The importance of this problem for the urban planner is twofold. On the one hand, if environmental factors contribute significantly to chronic anxiety or increased vulnerability to mental illness, then those preventive measures can be taken which would result in a reduction in the excessive demand for expensive psychiatric services. A second interest lies in the theoretical significance of the case. As the review of the literature in the field of community mental health has indicated, there is a gap in the development of practice knowledge relating mental illness to social-structural phenomena in ways that suggest structural solutions. A study that conceptualizes such solutions will help fill an important theoretical void.

20 Morris Rosenberg, *Society and the Adolescent Self-Image* (Princeton, N.J.: Princeton University Press, 1965).
21 *Ibid.*, p. 4.
22 *Ibid.*, p. 22.

Conceptualization of the problem   Rosenberg is primarily interested in self-esteem, that is the extent to which one's attitude about self is positive or negative. Does the individual have a favorable or unfavorable opinion of himself? Does he consider himself worthy or unworthy?

Rosenberg speculates that self-esteem is influenced to a large extent by the social factors in one's environment. Among these is the esteem with which one's group is held in the larger society.

> *For one thing, the hypothesis has been advanced that if groups are differentially esteemed in the broader society, then group members who internalize this value system may judge themselves accordingly. . . . A related point is that membership in a minority group in one's neighborhood—especially among children—may produce exclusion and rejection, and through the medium of reflected appraisals, feelings of inadequacy.*[23]

Thus Rosenberg postulates two aspects of the social environment that may affect self-esteem: (1) the degree of acceptance or rejection of a group within the larger society, and (2) the minority group status of the child in the neighborhood in which he grows up.

Self-esteem in this study is measured by a self-administered questionnaire containing a ten-item Guttman scale that was demonstrated to have "satisfactory reproducibility and scaleability." The validity of this test was measured in a pretest of 50 volunteers in which the scores correlated strongly with the independent ratings for depression on the Leary scales. They were also correlated with a list of 14 psychosomatic symptoms used by the U.S. Army in World War II to distinguish soldiers whose psychological malfunctioning required hospitalization. They were further validated against sociometric studies of 272 seniors from two high schools in Washington D.C. Rosenberg concludes "this scale is internally reliable and unidimensional and appears to have face validity."[24]

In summarizing the meaning of the concept as operationalized, Rosenberg reports:

> *When we speak of high self-esteem, then, we shall simply mean that the individual respects himself. . . ; he does not necessarily consider himself better than others. . . ; he recognizes his limitations and expects to grow and improve.*
>
> *Low self-esteem, on the other hand, implies self-rejection, self-dissatisfaction, self-contempt. . . . The self picture is disagreeable, and he wishes it were otherwise.*[25]

23 *Ibid.*, p. 13.
24 *Ibid.*, p. 30.
25 *Ibid.*, p. 31.

The study was made of a sample of 5,024 juniors and seniors from ten high schools drawn randomly from all public high schools in the state of New York. New York was chosen as the universe because it has a relatively heterogeneous population. The sample is random with respect to the high schools but not necessarily with the individual students. This sample excludes parochial and private school students, dropouts prior to their junior year, and absentees on the day on which the data were collected. The questionnaire was administered in the classroom by teachers. The students rated the test at the conclusion of the period as interesting and devoid of difficulty.

With respect to the first hypothesis regarding the impact of the general esteem of the subgroup of which an individual is a member, the predicted effect was not substantiated by the findings.

As an overall pattern, our data do not lend strong support to the stratification hypothesis. We have seen that the social prestige of a nationality or religious group is generally unrelated to the self-acceptance of its members.[26]

For example, of the three religious groups, Jews had the highest percentage of students with high self-esteem, 53 percent, while Catholics and Protestants had equal percentages, 43 percent.

However, the lack of any effect of the prestige of the group in the broader society, Rosenberg goes on to point out, does not exhaust the ill effects of being socially defined and treated as a minority group member.

The apparent contradiction arises from the failure to specify the effective interpersonal environment of the individual. Particularly in childhood, when the fundamental structure of personality is being formed, a more important interpersonal environment than the total society is a tiny segment of it, namely the neighborhood.[27]

As a test of this effect Rosenberg proposed the question, "Is there a discrepancy between, or concordance of, the individual's social characteristics and those of the population by which he is immediately surrounded?"[28]

This second hypothesis was tested by analyzing the self-esteem ratings of his sample with respect to the concordance or discordance of the

26 *Ibid.,* p. 61.
27 *Ibid.,* p. 64.
28 *Ibid.,* p. 64.

respondent's religion with the religious faith that predominated in the neighborhood in which he grew up.

This analysis was accomplished by asking the respondents to recall the neighborhood in which they lived the longest and to estimate in general terms the religious affiliation of most of the people in that neighborhood. The respondents were asked to classify their answer in one of the following three categories: (1) almost all of the families in the neighborhood were of a specified religion, (2) about half were of one religion and half were of another, (3) about three-quarters were of one religion and one-quarter were of another.

A consonant neighborhood was one in which at least three-quarters of the residents were of the same religion as the respondent. Mixed neighborhoods were those in which approximately one-half were of the same religion. Dissonant neighborhoods were those in which one-quarter or less were of the same religion as the respondent.

The findings of this analysis show that there was indeed a difference in the prevalence of low self-esteem among adolescents who as children lived in dissonant neighborhoods. For Catholics it was 41 percent compared to 29 percent in mixed or consonant neighborhoods. For Protestants the difference was 31 percent to 25 percent, and for Jews it was 29 percent to 18 percent. Similar differences occurred with respect to the prevalence of psychosomatic symptoms. While the differences are not large or statistically significant in every case, they are perfectly consistent. The graphing of such findings appears in Figure 5.

It is important to note that there is no clear difference in emotional distress between adolescents who were raised in neighborhoods in which almost all residents were coreligionists and those raised in neighborhoods in which only one-half were coreligionists.

> *This result would suggest that whether everyone in the neighborhood is of one's group is less important than whether there are enough of them to give one social support, a feeling of belonging. . . . It is only when the individual is in the distinct minority, when it is impossible for him to restrict his association to members of his own group, that the deleterious psychological consequences of the dissonant religious context become evident.*[29]

Rosenberg carries his analysis one step further to suggest the dynamics by which the minority child's self-esteem is adversely affected. The child isolated from his religious group faces his environment without group support. The majority group defines a minority group member as

29 *Ibid.,* p. 68.

FIGURE 5:

Effect of religious dissonance in neighborhood of
childhood on adolescent self-image.

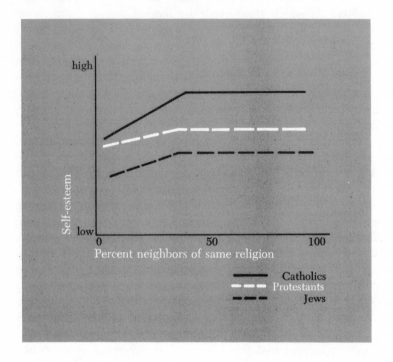

different and inferior. The majority group rejects the minority group
member from participation, taunts him, and subjects him to the infinite
variety of acts of cruelty of which children are capable.

Respondents were asked, "When you were a child, were you ever
teased, left out of things, or called names by other children because of
your religion?" The result showed a marked difference between consonant and dissonant neighborhoods. For Catholics, 22 percent living in
dissonant neighborhoods reported being subjected to such acts while
only 5 percent in consonant or mixed neighborhoods so responded. For
Protestants, the difference was 22 percent to 6 percent, for Jews it was
48 percent to 26 percent.

When the effect of a dissonant context on self-esteem was standard-
ized for whether or not the respondent had experienced prejudice, five
out of the six comparisons showed a reduced relationship. However, the
relationships did not completely disappear. Rosenberg concludes:

The experience of discrimination thus appears to contribute to the psychological consequences of contextual dissonance but does not account for them completely. To be reared in a dissonant context thus reflects more than the experience of being taunted, ridiculed, attacked, or excluded on the basis of one's group affiliation. What is also probably involved is the insecurity which stems from lack of integration in the group, issuing from a feeling of social isolation, a sense of being "different," an absence of "belongingness."[30]

Social structure   Again, the case under review focuses on the system of social relationships that prevails in the neighborhood. In this case, it is confined to the peer group of the child. The structural feature that is at issue is the composition of the neighborhood in regard to religious affiliation. When the statuses of this structure are filled with actors of the same religious persuasion, the relationships are mutually supporting and esteem-enhancing. When they are filled with actors from other religious faiths, the peer relationships are rejecting and self-degrading. The strategy of change in this case is the membership composition of the structure, rather than the status-role elements of the structure.

As Rosenberg frequently points out, the implications are equally applicable to other subcultural differences, such as race, in which the majority-minority relations are based on rejection or valuations of inferiority.

Tool of intervention   Intervention in this particular case must occur at some point in the process that determines the residential composition of a neighborhood. However, it is much more difficult to influence the family composition of neighborhoods than it is the tenant patterns in large apartment complexes.

Two handicaps prevail: (1) there is no central control over tenant occupancy and (2) public policy is in opposition to racial or religious patterning. With respect to the latter, it should be pointed out that the Rosenberg study does not imply segregation. Mixed neighborhoods are conducive to the development of positive self-images among children. The point of the study is that the isolation of children into distinct minority positions is to be avoided.

This case suggests, on the one hand, the rejection of the goal frequently voiced of dispersing the ghetto throughout the metropolitan

30 *Ibid.*, pp. 71f.

area. Programs that result in the break up of ethnic neighborhoods should be avoided. On the other hand, minority groups should be encouraged to live in close proximity. This objective can be achieved in a positive way by the purposeful location in close proximity of community facilities that have particular significance for religious or racial minorities. Public policies have some control over such locations through master planning for neighborhood facilities and through federal funds for the construction of community facilities. The strengthening of minority group neighborhoods can also be encouraged by "community control" of schools, local businesses, and similar services.

Residual alternatives   The obvious alternative to this case of social-structural change is the familiar pattern of psychiatric treatment for emotionally disturbed children. This study does not presume to eliminate such need.

> *Our data do not suggest that the dissonant social context is a powerful factor in producing these signs of emotional disturbance, but the consistency of the results suggest that it may be a real factor. We doubt whether the dissonant context often produces these psychological consequences independently of other factors. Rather, we would be inclined to assume that its main influence is exercised upon those already predisposed to psychological disturbance; those standing near the cliff are pushed ever closer to it or actually over it.*[31]

However, the report does illustrate one contribution which a social-structural perspective can make to the understanding of mental illness and its reduction.

Implications for social policy   This case has implications for the treatment of racism. The ability of blacks to achieve equality in our society may indeed be enhanced by the extent to which they are able to band together and provide the group support necessary to protect themselves from the pernicious effects of majority prejudice. Black power, rather than a source of danger, is a source of social strength in that it counteracts the dependency and self-defeatism that accompanies the rejected, low status ascribed to minority groups in our society.

The argument for minority grouping is not necessarily in conflict with the Deutsch and Collins integration model. In the latter, Negroes

---

31 *Ibid.*, p. 78.

accounted for 40 percent of integrated projects. As long as the mixture is fairly even, benefits will accrue to both groups—for the majority, an opportunity to discard false prejudices; for the minority, sufficient support from group identification to fend off rejection by the majority, and to project a positive self-image onto the minority.

Chapter 4

CASE STUDIES IN
SOCIAL-STRUCTURAL CHANGE:
THROUGH CHANGES IN ROLES

The present chapter deals with cases involving some change in the roles of a system of social relationships. The preceding chapter, in contrast, dealt with changes in the membership of such structures assuming that the structures were held constant in so far as the planned intervention was concerned.

The question arises as to whether changes in role composition can be considered independently of changes in the pattern of statuses. Chapter 2 revealed that most authorities consider roles and statuses to be inseparable phenomena, that it is impossible to deal with one without involving the other. In this sense, it is inconceivable that a change in a given status of a given structure would not result in an alteration in the accompanying roles, and vice versa.

Although the concepts of role and status represent inseparable characteristics of a common phenomenon, we will demonstrate through the cases in this chapter that they constitute separate means of achieving structural change. That is to say, structural change can be promulgated either by attacking the role definitions of a given structure or by altering the statuses that comprise the structure, even though a change in one will invariably result in a change in the other. The redefinition of functions in a given system constitutes a direct attack on the role aspect of social structure, as in the case of the introduction of neighborhood aides in the community action programs. Conversely, when rights or obligations are redistributed, the structure is attacked through its status arrangements as in the case of income redistribution, or the reallocation of salaries among positions within an organizational system.

Thus, in this chapter we will focus our attention on changes in structures which are achieved through role redefinition irrespective of status rearrangements, recognizing that the result of one intervention will involve the other. Examples of structural change accomplished through status rearrangement will be analyzed in Chapter 5.

JANE JACOBS: SAFETY ON THE STREETS

With the work of Jane Jacobs, the analysis of social-structural change turns to alterations in the pattern of roles in a social situation.[1] The Jacobs' case is more complex than the former cases, but it lends itself well to a structural argument. Its complexity reflects a more inclusive grasp of reality in contrast to the former cases which, based on empirical research, were of necessity more abstract and simplified.

Social problem   The social problem with which Jacobs is concerned is the lack of safety on the streets. There has been much talk lately of the increase of crime in cities—a rather heterogeneous and complicated set of phenomena. However, Jacobs is concerned with only one aspect of crime—the seemingly random acts of larceny, vandalism, and personal assault that are reported so frequently in the pages of the daily newspapers. She is not dealing with organized crime or acts of violence that can be interpreted as forms of social protest.

The problem of safety on the streets is a major one in most cities and therefore of central concern to urban planners. The problem of adherence to socially accepted norms of behavior increases with urbanization and is realistic quite apart from current efforts to exploit the issue for political purposes. The ability of experts to erect beautiful physical reconstructions of central city areas, while being seemingly impotent in the face of serious breakdown in normal means of social control, represents one of the most dramatic failures of urban planners to date.

1 Jane Jacobs, *The Death and Life of Great American Cities* (New York: Random House, Inc., 1961).

Conceptualization of the problem   Jane Jacobs' work contains an innovative approach to understanding this problem. It is particularly important because her approach is based on a realistic assessment of the social nature of cities. It recognizes that large cities are not small communities; the informal methods of gossip and approval, effective in the latter will not work in the former. The city is inhabited by strangers which is both its strength and its source of difficulty. People seek the greater freedom afforded by the relative anonymity of city public life. But this freedom is purchased at a price: it weakens the normal processes of social control. Jacobs builds a theory of social control that is based on the acceptance of "strangers" and "city public life."

Jacobs' reasoning is based on a sociological truism, long since demonstrated by Durkheim.

> *The first thing to understand is that the public peace—the sidewalk and street peace—of cities is not kept primarily by the police, necessary as police are. It is kept primarily by an intricate, almost unconscious network of voluntary controls and standards among the people themselves, and enforced by the people themselves.*[2]

The argument that Jacobs makes with respect to the social context of the street as a deterrent to crime involves a number of considerations, only some of which are relevant to this analysis. In essence her argument is that busy streets are safe streets because constant activity on the street provides a natural attraction to watchers to provide "eyes on the street." It is this natural form of surveillance that is the most effective deterrent to crime.

How is a constant flow of activity created on the street? By a variety of land uses which attracts pedestrians at different times throughout the day and night and creates a criss-cross of traffic; in sociological terms, a street on which many roles are played—the resident sweeping his front step, the shopper buying goods, the worker going to and from his job, the children at play, the pleasure seeker on his way to a place of diversion.

However, activity on the street is not enough to turn the watchers into enforcers of the peace in the event of an attempted disorder.

> *Action usually requires, to be sure, a certain self-assurance about the actor's proprietorship of the street and the support he will get if necessary. . . .*[3]

Thus, a sense of proprietorship in the mind which lies behind the "eyes on the street" is necessary before surveillance can escalate into intervention.

2 *Ibid.*, p. 32.
3 *Ibid.*, p. 38.

But how does this sense of proprietorship arise? Jacobs' explanation is not altogether clear. She speaks of its arising from "a web of public respect and trust," a "feeling for the public identity of people."[4] Such feelings come from repetitive, superficial sidewalk contacts between different people in different roles, neighbors exchanging greetings while walking their dogs, the newsboy and his regular customers, those who frequent the neighborhood bar. The implication is that a sense of proprietorship arises in any individual who plays a diversity of roles in a given street, such as maintaining a home, raising children, shopping, going to work, having friends. Such proprietors are in contrast to strangers who come into the neighborhood without getting involved in the web of public identity, who presumably play only one role on the street.

The stage is now set for a social-compositional analysis. Public safety on the streets is maintained, not only by a diversity of roles enacted on the street to attract "eyes on the street," but also by a diversity of roles enacted by a given individual user of the street to create a sense of proprietorship and a web of public support.

This delicate relationship between the diversity of roles enacted on the street and the diversity of roles enacted by a given individual on the street can be clarified by the technique of social-compositional analysis. Figure 6 shows schematically what might be expected. Proprietors have a higher probability of watching the street than strangers. But as the diversity of roles enacted on the street increases, the probability of both groups watching the street increases.

However, there is an interaction effect between strangers and proprietors. Although the presence of proprietors among those who watch the streets is essential, the addition of strangers enhances their function of peace keeping. Strangers on the street not only add additional eyes, but they induce the proprietors to watch what is going on. "Once a street...has a basic supply of activity and eyes, the more strangers the merrier."

But not quite. For if strangers come to predominate, then no amount of diversified role playing will keep the peace.

The high-rent tenants, most of whom are so transient we cannot even keep track of their faces, have not the remotest idea of who takes care of their street, or how. A city neighborhood can absorb and protect a substantial number of these birds of passage, as our neighborhood does. But if and when the neighborhood finally becomes them, they will gradually find the streets less secure....[5]

4 *Ibid.*, p. 56.
5 *Ibid.*, p. 39.

FIGURE 6:

Effect of role composition on safety of the streets.

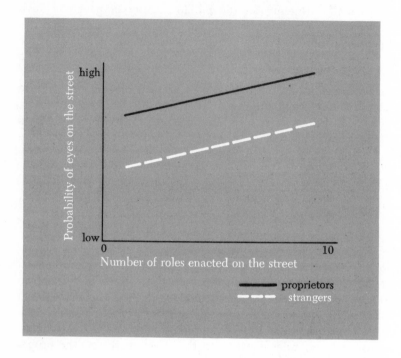

Yet strangers will help keep the peace when there is a network of proprietors to initiate the action.

Figure 7 shows the effect of interaction. Proprietors have a high probability of watching the street even in the absence of strangers, but as strangers become users of the street, the probability of steet watching among proprietors increases until strangers come to predominate, and then it falls off to zero. Strangers on the other hand start with a lower but significant probability of street watching, which declines more linearly with the increase preponderance of strangers among street users.

Social structure   The system of social relationships conceptualized in this case is the "web of public street life," the informal network of superficial relationships that exists among regular users of a city street. The structure consists of two statuses: strangers and proprietors. The former are defined in terms of their having only one role on the street, while the latter have multiple roles.

FIGURE 7:
Effect of membership composition on safety on streets.

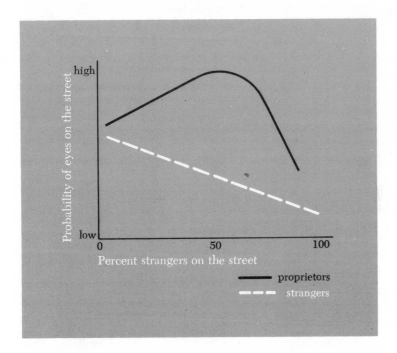

It is the role structure of the system of social relations that is the heart of this analysis. Jacobs' hypothesis of how to achieve safety on the streets rests on the number of roles played by street users necessary to maintain the balance between strangers and proprietors.

This is a case of changing the elements of the structure rather than changing the membership of the structure. The cases discussed in Chapter 3 involved altering the membership composition with respect to some attribute of individuals: in the first case it was race, in the second case it was age, in the third case it was religion. In this case, the structural phenomena being altered are the roles of actors in the system.

Tool of intervention   An advantage of the Jacobs' analysis is its direct grounding in the practical business of city planning. Jacobs posits a very direct connection between land use controls and the social structure of the urban street. Rather than segregating land uses, as city planners were wont to do, Jacobs advocates a rich mixture of land uses including residential, entertainment, commercial, and even industrial. Land use controls, such as zoning and building permits, are accepted tools used by city planners in shaping the face of cities.

Again, as in the case of former tools, the availability of land use controls to the urban planner is not tantamount to his ability to change a social situation. There are a number of countervailing influences on the determination of land use: those of builders, businessmen, and other special interest groups whose purposes may or may not be compatible with those of the planner. Nevertheless the tool is specific, is available, and constitutes an appropriate point of intervention.

Residual alternatives   The residual alternatives to social-structural change in this particular case are fairly obvious. For example, greater police protection and surveillance seems to be the present hallmark of proposals for public action. However, as Jacobs points out, the police are not the ultimate source of social control.

Similarly, social work as a profession concerned with the field of crime and corrections, has tended to focus its efforts on individual actors in the situation, in this case the perpetrators of the crime. For example, group work services have been organized to work with delinquent youth in urban neighborhoods to redirect their interests and frustrations into socially constructive channels. Such an approach may be necessary in any event. However, in lieu of a social structure that prevents such acting-out behavior, working only with the criminals involved on a one-to-one basis is an interminable task.

Implications for social policy   As with any pointed attack on established systems of thought or action, Jacobs' prescriptions for the ills of the American city have come under strong attack, particularly from city planners whose traditional methods she maligned. Most of her critics focus on the physical implications of her analysis and completely ignore the social dimension of urban life that she brought to the fore.[6] Such critics decry the high density of population and the increase in land devoted to city streets implied in Jacobs' proposals. Others point out the economic infeasibility of attracting industry or other employment-producing enterprises into small locations interspersed throughout residential areas of the city.

More relevant to a social policy interest are criticisms pointing to a bias against poor people in Jacobs' proposals. The kind of land devel-

6 For a typical sampling of such criticisms see A. Melamed, *Journal of the American Institute of Planners*, Vol. 28, No. 2 (May 1962), 137–39; and Roger Starr, *Urban Choices: The City and Its Critics* (Baltimore, Md.: Penguin Books, Inc., 1967), pp. 102–3, 163–66.

opment she favors is relatively expensive. This criticism is hard to reconcile with the frequently expressed counter-argument that her proposals appeal only to low income ethnic groups who want to live that way, and that there are not enough such groups for every district in the city.

In terms of the very premises that Jacobs uses to arrive at her conclusions, more substantive criticisms are made. One of them has to do with the fact that some need exists for privacy even in the largest cities. Some open spaces, particularly parks, are sought out by city dwellers from time to time to escape the noise and crowding of city life and to find an atmosphere conducive to contemplation and privacy. Jacobs' argument that constant activity is the summum bonum of urban life has its obvious limitations.

Similarly, her assumption that proprietors are always protective of strangers who use their streets has recently encountered some negative evidence. In recent years the hippies who invaded the North End of Boston—one of Jacobs' prime examples of a neighborhood with safe city streets—have been victimized by the very neighborhood proprietors who were supposed to be their protectors. Such a turn of events seemingly represents a serious challenge to the Jacobs premise.

But does it? It is one thing for strangers who conform to the basic norms to which North Enders ascribe, to walk through the neighborhood and use its facilities. It is quite a different matter when such strangers are people who by their dress and behavior challenge the norms of the community and represent failures in the eyes of the local society. The hippies constituted a threat to the way of life in the North End, whereas the type of strangers Jacobs refers to are neutral, at most, in their challenge to local customs. This is the familiar phenomenon of smalltown intolerance of "foreigners."

We have come full circle in the argument. We started out by noting that the means of social control typical of the small village is for members to punish nonconformers directly, whereas in the city an anonymity protects the deviant from such retribution on the part of fellow citizens. In reconstructing a system of public street life to provide informal means of social control, it must be recognized that, just as in the case of the small town, this control can be used to exploit the rights of nonconformers as well as to protect the lives of the innocent. Thus, Jacobs' prescriptions regarding safety on the streets hold true only when the strangers are neutral with respect to the basic value system of the proprietors of that street, and become self-defeating when those strangers represent invaders who may take over the street, or persons who threaten the way of life of the indigenous proprietors of the streets.

There are distinct limitations to the applicability of Jacobs' thesis. Not all areas of the city can be reconstructed in terms of neat little urban villages. However, attention to social control functions of the social structure of a given area will enhance the ability of planners to reduce crime through a normal process, as well as to identify those areas of the city for which artificial measures must be devised.

PEARL AND RIESSMAN: NEW CAREERS FOR THE POOR

The study of formal organizations provides a rich field for the analysis of social-structural change. Formal organizations have clear boundaries and therefore are easily identified. Control over their structure and functioning tends to be clearly defined and accessible. For these reasons, organizational design constitutes a natural subject for social planning.

Social scientists have not always looked at organizational behavior in systemic terms. As Katz points out:

> *The major error in dealing with problems of organizational change...is to disregard the systemic properties of the organization and to confuse individual change with modifications in organizational variables. It is common practice to pull foremen or officials out of their organizational roles and give them training in human relations. They then return to their customary positions with the same role expectations from their subordinates, the same pressures from their superiors, and the same functions to perform as before their special training.*[7]

Industrial organizations have been a prolific subject for study by sociologists and psychologists. Management has promoted such studies in order to increase worker productivity. Industries lend themselves to an analysis of role changes since they can be easily analyzed in terms of functions performed to create a given product.

There are several studies on role structures in industrial settings, for the most part focused on specialization versus diversification of roles or work teams. The institution of the "assembly line" in a mass production plant is an obvious case in point.[8] However these studies have little direct relevance to the purposes of this analysis. Therefore, we shall attempt to find cases in which this interest in the structure of work roles is applied to the social services.

Social problem   The case that lends itself to such an analysis is the proposal by Arthur Pearl and Frank Riessman to create new careers

---

7 Daniel Katz and Robert L. Kahn, *The Social Psychology of Organizations* (New York: John Wiley & Sons, Inc., 1966), p. 390.
8 For examples of such studies see Daniel Katz, *op. cit.*, pp. 425–51.

for the poor.[9] The problem with which Pearl and Riessman deal is the inability of health, welfare, and educational agencies to engage their target populations in service when such populations constitute a distinct subcultural group based on class or ethnicity. The organization with which they deal is the service agency. The "product" is a person who has successfully completed treatment, or, to put it more crudely, is "a closed case." The principal roles in this organization are the professional practitioner and the client or applicant for service.

The extent to which those who are most in need of assistance actually benefit from public social services has long been a public concern. It underlies much of the rationale for the demonstration projects funded by the President's Committee on Juvenile Delinquency and the Community Action Programs under the Economic Opportunity Act. Indeed, one of the justifications of the citizen participation clause in the Act was that it would provide a means for closing this gap.

Conceptualization of the problem   Running through the Pearl and Riessman argument are two somewhat contradictory themes. One theme attributes the crisis in the quality and availability of human services, particularly in the inner city, to manpower practices—the insufficient supply of professional personnel, and the use of professionals to perform nonprofessional duties. This argument leads them to advocate a program of new careers for the poor. Such a program involves defining out of the professional's role those functions which do not require professional training and assigning them to nonprofessional, less expensive personnel. This argument is not particularly of interest to us here for it is non-systemic in nature, it does not relate the crisis in service delivery to the system of social relationships existing among practitioners and their target population. It is rather paternalistic at best, and contradicts their other theme.

The second theme which the authors use in diagnosing the crisis in the delivery of services is based on the notion that there are some functions in the provision of service which nonindigenous, professional personnel are not equipped to perform. The role of the professional is (1) to further the objectives of his agency, and (2) to pursue and expand the body of knowledge upon which his professional practice rests. These two functions often place him in conflict with the immediate needs of the target population. When a client's demands do not fall within the definition of the agency's resources, or when his particular problem does

9 Arthur Pearl and Frank Riessman, *New Careers For the Poor* (New York: The Free Press, 1965); *see also* S. M. Miller and Frank Riessman, *Social Class and Social Policy* (New York: Basic Books, Inc., Publishers, 1968).

not fall within the professional competence of the practitioner, the client's requests are usually denied. This view is consistent with the fact that professionals spend increasing amounts of time in consultation, teaching, writing, and administration, a fact that may enhance the delivery of service but is not a substitute for it.

The authors argue for a new role or function to be played in service agencies. This function is representation of the client and his interests in opposition to those of the agency. The role is similar to that of the court appointed defense attorney.

Pearl and Riessman describe this function in several different service settings. For example, in the field of education they discuss the "dialect game." Efforts by children of a particular subculture to communicate in their own dialect may be rejected by middle-class teachers. The "teacher aide" who is indigenous to that subculture can prevent this rejection by communicating with the student in his own dialect, as well as with the teacher in her dialect. After self-confidence is established, the aide can help teach the student his new language.

In the field of mental health, the authors describe a role called the "helper therapist." This role is played by a person who is recruited out of the ranks of the target population, either because he is not as severely ill as the rest of the group or because he has recently recovered. Such persons act as role models for recovery. Through identification with a common symptom and social background, they increase the client's motivation to use the treatment services. In addition, being a helper therapist may be instrumental in one's own recovery. The authors point to studies which indicate that persons become committed to a course of action through advocating it. Alcoholics Anonymous is a classic case in point.

In terms of a welfare agency, the nonprofessional role is one of advocating the needs and rights of clients in relation to the agency's resources. The effect of this role is to counterbalance the professional's tendency to conform to agency policy in determining eligibility for assistance. The nonprofessional person identifies with the client. The target population represents his peer group and is the object of his primary loyalty. In contrast, the professional's peer group is composed of fellow professionals, and his primary loyalty is to his profession and his agency. Anyone who has seen a representative of the Welfare Rights Organization advocate the needs of a welfare recipient before a welfare department caseworker knows the value of this function.

Miller and Riessman identify this role as "the expediter" in social service agencies. They see the role in the tradition of the now extinct "ward healer" who was able to secure service from community resources for his constituents. They define "the expediter" in terms of several functions. (1) He is an *interpreter* of the particular subcultural meanings or attitudes expressed by the client. (2) He is a *negotiator* who breaks through agency red tape to secure his client's requests. (3) He is an *attorney* who advocates the rights of his client. (4) He is an *educator* who informs a client of the kinds of services available to him. (5) He is an *instructor* who teaches the client the best way of getting a particular service and how to use it. (6) He is a *helper* by assisting the client in articulating his problem and by providing support in seeking solutions.

Social structure   This analysis of the failure of agencies to provide service to their target populations is set in the context of the service agency as a social system. The principal elements in this analysis are the roles played by professional staff who act as gatekeepers of the agency and clients or applicants who seek its service. The failure of the agency to engage the target population in service is attributed to the confinement of the agency's structure to these two roles.

The analysis has used the terms client and target population interchangeably, even though they refer to different statuses in relation to the agency system. The former denotes persons who have been accepted by the agency for service, while the latter designates the aggregate of persons in the population at large who exhibit the conditions that the agency purports to serve. Whether inside the agency or not, the phenomenon of requesting assistance has a basic similarity, that of negotiating an agreement to provide assistance to which one presumably is entitled.

To increase the agency's ability to serve its target population, the authors propose the introduction of a new role, that of expediter—someone who is neither professional nor client. The assumption is that the expediter can increase the number of agreements reached, and thereby increase the agency's rate of admitting or terminating appropriate cases. As members of the target population become more successful in receiving needed services, their experience will stimulate other members of the target population to seek the agency's assistance. Social-structural change is achieved in this case through a change in the composition of the roles rather than the membership. The argument in this approach is that the failure to receive service is not a function of the client's attitudes, knowledge, or ability, but rather the process whereby the system engages clients.

In introducing this new role, it is clear that the behavior of the client as well as the professional is affected. The client becomes more self-assured and aggressive in seeking assistance. The professional's ability to turn down requests for service is compromised by the legitimized pressure exerted by the expediter.

In summarizing the effect of this structural change on service delivery, Pearl and Riessman refer to the particular expertise of indigenous personnel.

It is possible that indigenous workers' skills emanate from the roles they play in relation to their clients, rather than their personalities. In other words it may not be who they are, but rather what they do and how they do it that is decisive. The reason for the success of the non-professional may lie in the fact that he is able to do what professionals don't do.[10]

In graphing the compositional effect in this case, we discover an interesting fact (see Figure 8). The independent variable is the creation of an expediter service role. The dependent variable is the rate of

FIGURE 8
Effect of expediter role on rate of admissions (case closings) for target population.

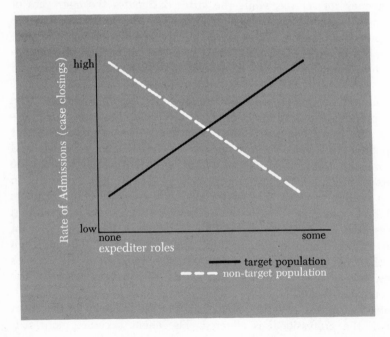

10 Arthur Pearl and Frank Riessman, *op. cit.*, p. 90.

admissions or case closings. The individuals on whom this structural change is expected to have a desirable effect are members of the target population.

But since a compositional analysis requires examination of all persons exposed to the structural change, not just those for whom it is to have a desirable effect, who constitutes the contrasting group? It must consist of persons seeking service who are not members of the target population. While this contrast may appear logically absurd, in actual practice it has considerable validity. In order to justify their existence, agencies must show a full caseload. When the appropriate clientele do not apply or are not accepted for service, others are served. Thus, the agency falls into the trap of maintaining a full caseload while at the same time trying to increase clientele from the target population, practices which may be contradictory.

Assuming a fixed budget, the graphing of the effect of this structural change would indicate intersecting curves; as admissions from the target population increase, admissions from the nontarget population decrease.

Tool of intervention   The tool of intervention in this particular case is administrative regulations or policies. The structural change requires a revamping of the job descriptions and chart of organization of a service agency. Such changes would inevitably involve alterations in the agency's budget, as well as new procedures for staff recruitment, training, and supervision. All of these tools of intervention are usually exercised by agency administrators. This fact suggests a natural alignment between social planning and administration.

Residual alternatives   Even before the advent of Community Action Programs, social agencies were concerned about their ability to reach target populations, particularly those consisting of diverse socio-economic and ethnic groups. However, efforts to improve outreach tended to be based on the assumption that the target population lacked information or agency offices were geographically inaccessible. Public information efforts were launched, directories of services were distributed, telephone information and referral services were established, and agencies experimented with opening branch offices.

However, as Herbert Gans has articulated, the mere location of a service or facility in the target area does not assure that it will be used by the target popoulation.[11] Utilization depends on the extent to which the service becomes a part of the social system of that population. Pearl

11 Herbert Gans, *People and Place*, p. 6.

and Riessman provide one approach for achieving that objective by restructuring the roles of a service agency.

Implications for social policy   The use of neighborhood aides or nonprofessional workers as client advocates inside the agency has received increasing attention and popularity since the advent of the war on poverty. However, there is not much evidence about the impact such incursions have had on the delivery of service to target populations.

A follow-up study of an experimental prenatal clinic designed to reduce neonatal mortality by serving women who had never received prenatal care during pregnancy showed positive results.[12] The clinic was established in a low-income, predominantly black section of North Philadelphia, with a high rate of neonatal mortality. It resulted from the combined efforts of local hospitals, churches, social agencies, and neighborhood citizen groups. Local residents were used in a variety of semi-professional roles in the clinic. In contrast to this volunteer effort, the City of Philadelphia established a prenatal clinic in a similar neighborhood in West Philadelphia using traditional professional staff. After a year of operation, the North Philadelphia clinic showed dramatic results in reaching its target population. Almost all of its cases were women who had first pregnancies or had not received prenatal care during previous pregnancies. The West Philadelphia clinic languished for clients. All of those who came had received prenatal care previously.

The Pearl and Riessman proposal is questionable as a long-term solution to the problem of service delivery to subcultural populations. In a sense it is a transitional solution. The authors themselves recognize the natural ambiguity that arises in the case of the role of the nonprofessional in a professionally dominated agency. Out of self-interest in upward mobility there is a tendency for the indigenous worker to identify with the professional, and thereby lose value as a client advocate.[13]

A more realistic model in the long run may be one in which representatives of the target population or ethnic groups involved occupy the professional roles. Still another alternative is suggested by the movement for "community control." Once a service agency is under the control of those who identify with the target population involved, the professional-client relationship may become more productive without the need for an expediter.

---

12 Robert R. Mayer, *The Role of Volunteers in Effecting the Use of Health Clinic Services in a Community of Intense Social and Economic Needs* (Philadelphia, Pa.: Philadelphia Health and Welfare Council, 1959).

13 This tendency was foreseen in the experience of Mobilization For Youth as reflected in an analysis of its homemaker service program. See Charles F. Grosser, "Class Orientation of the Indigenous Staff," in *Community Action Against Poverty*, pp. 208–28.

SHAPIRO: COMMUNITY OF THE ALONE

The final case in this Chapter is somewhat different in style from the rest.[14] It results neither from a theoretically-based piece of research, nor from a clearly articulated conceptual framework. Rather it is taken from the experience of a social worker, Joan H. Shapiro, reported in a professional journal on social work. The case, however, so clearly demonstrates the social-structural model of problem solving that it is useful here. It has the advantage of being closer to practice than theory, and thus provides a needed balance to earlier cases which are closer to theory than practice. Because of this stylistic difference, some of the missing pieces in the conceptualization will have to be provided by deduction from the general theoretical orientation of this analysis.

Social problem   The "community of the alone" refers to the single, unattached individuals who inhabit cheap rooming houses near the central business districts of most cities. According to Shapiro, such individuals are a social problem for two reasons. In the first place they are, for the most part, economically dependent and socially deviant members of society. Among them there is a high degree of welfare recipiency, alcoholism, drug addiction, and chronic illness. Such a population is a social problem because its members require exceptional care and are dependent on community resources for obtaining it.

In the second place, such individuals are a threat to their surrounding neighborhoods. In the case under discussion, there was a high incidence of theft and mugging in the neighborhood attributed to residents of a rooming house, causing neighborhood groups to apply pressure on the city to close down the house. The City stationed a policeman on the corner where the building was located to protect the neighborhood from such acts.

Therefore, single unattached individuals who inhabit cheap rooming houses are a problem because of the inadequate care being received by the individuals involved, as well as their adverse effect on the surrounding neighborhood.

Rooming houses with such a constituency are not rare. They comprise a significant section of most central cities across the nation, and invariably are in the path of the bulldozers that are "renewing" the downtown core. Most urban renewal projects come face-to-face with this phenomenon often known as skid row.[15]

14 Joan H. Shapiro, "Single-Room Occupancy: Community of the Alone," *Social Work*, 11 (October 1966) 24–34.
15 Donald Bogue, *Skid Row in American Cities* (Chicago: University of Chicago, Community and Family Study Center, 1963).

In New York City alone there are 600 single-room occupancy buildings licensed by the City housing a population of 50,000 people. The
persons involved constitute a large portion of the poor population.[16]
They are not sick or deviant enough for institutionalization, nor well
enough to be absorbed into the mainstream of the community. They
suffer from loneliness, untreated illness, hunger, and sporadic outbursts
of violence.

Conceptualization of the problem   Shapiro's approach to solving
this problem developed from a traditional service delivery point of view.
She was assigned by a local psychiatric hospital to work with the tenants
and the management of a given rooming house in an effort to refer the
occupants to health and welfare agencies for rehabilitation. As Shapiro
became engaged with her clients, she perceived that they had already
found a solution to their problem—that through their living together
in the rooming house they had formed the rudiments of a system of
social relationships that provided mutual support, self-help, and indigenous social welfare institutions.

At the first meeting with the tenants to discuss their concerns, she
observed their informal means of social control. Individuals who were
overt troublemakers were put down by other tenants or muscled-off
into a corner where they could not cause trouble. The tenants themselves
established permissible limits of behavior in the recreation room that
was provided at their request.

There was a very clear sense of boundary to this system. Every tenant
was aware of the strong negative attitudes on the part of the public
toward the building. Neighbors avoided sitting on the stoop, and the
policeman on the corner was an ever-present reminder. Shapiro reported
"their passive watchfulness toward outsiders which masked anger and
fear." They patronized only those stores whose owners were friendly.
The park, one-half block away, was seldom used; it was considered the
territory of middle-class neighborhood residents. The radius of their
behavior was less than two blocks—many spent days on end without
going outside the building. Some did not even know how to use a bus
or subway to get to more distant parts of the city. A trip to a clinic was
a cause for major anxiety. They did not vote, read newspapers, go to
church, or belong to volunteer organizations. "As rejects from the larger
society, the tenants in turn actively repudiated its concerns and values."[17]

There was ample evidence of internal institutions to meet the needs
of its members. An older woman, a welfare recipient, cared for the

16 Shapiro, "Single-Room Occupancy," p. 32.
17 *Ibid.*, p. 30.

bedridden tenants. She cleaned and cooked for them without remuneration. In this sense she served as a visiting nurse and homemaker. A young man who received excess tranquilizers from a doctor dispensed them one at a time to fellow tenants with a one-hour sympathy session in which he listened to their problems. A woman alcoholic provided emergency meals for those who had inadequate income or could not budget their monthly welfare checks. In return, others would share a bottle of spirits with her when she was without. A strong ex-boxer with a gentle personality kept the peace.

Ties to primary family were tenuous or absent. However, all but a few were intimately involved with others. There was no evidence of anomie or reclusiveness as is sometimes posited. Only six among the one hundred inhabitants of the building were psychologically isolated.

Shapiro's efforts were devoted to supporting and enhancing this indigenous system. This was accomplished by fostering group decision making on the part of the tenants, and by relating primarily to the natural leaders within the system. As a result of group meetings, a recreation program was established on a regular basis including a library and movies. In addition, a community dining room was set up to serve meals bi-weekly on the eve of "check day" when residents were most hard-pressed. In terms of the rehabilitation program, a committee was selected by the tenants to encourage referrals and to accompany individual members to their clinic appointments.

The results of these efforts were mixed. Initially there was much cynicism about the individual's capacity for change. However, attitudes shifted to overt group approval of lessened drinking, clinic visits, or detoxification. This acceptance did not extend to those few who actually found employment; they were consistently ostracized. A visit to a psychological clinic received public acclaim, but "upward mobility threatened the group's unity in its negative stance toward the majority culture."[18]

The persons most intensively changed were those who participated most actively. Fifty-two tenants had successful major referrals to medical, psychiatric, welfare, or rehabilitation services. Some needed continuing support in their clinic visits. However, a large group remained unchanged except that they used the recreation program which drew an average attendance of forty-five. The dinner was the one continuous function that involved a large majority of the tenants.

Fifteen percent were not involved in any way. The number of recluses was small. Most of those uninvolved consisted of a group of self-sufficient young Puerto Rican men, and a group of fully employed blue collar workers.

18 *Ibid.*, p. 30.

An important outcome of the project was improved relations with the neighborhood.

During the fourth month of the program the special police post was cancelled owing to lack of complaints. This phase was marked by a general leveling off, both in program content and building atmosphere, and stabilization of the roles of various participants in recreation and rehabilitation parts of the program.[19]

Shapiro concludes with the following overall evaluation.

The general atmosphere of the building became more positive, many of the tenants having increased the number of their social relationships and their degree of protectiveness toward one another. The tenants' self-image changed to one of pride in themselves, their project, and their building.[20]

Social structure   The Shapiro case is focused primarily on the system of social relationships that exists among neighbors, treating the rooming house as a miniature neighborhood. The primary structural feature which accounts for the desired results in this case is the membership of that system based on social deviancy. However, significant alterations in statuses and roles also occurred.

Almost all of the tenants of the rooming house were social deviants of one form or another. Many came to the building as dischargees from some form of institutional care. Fifty-two percent of the population were alcoholic. Twenty-two percent were addicted to heroin or barbiturates. The women often engaged in prostitution to support their habit. Eleven percent exhibited grossly bizarre behavior or irrational communication. It was estimated that of this group, two percent were mentally retarded—they were treated as the "children" of the building. Thus, 90 percent of the inhabitants had some major psycho-social maladaptation.

Furthermore, the internal social structure of the rooming house was stratified by type of deviancy. It consisted of three substructures or primary groups based on common pathology: "winos," "junkies," and "mentals." "The pattern of relationships (within the house) took the form of well-defined, matriarchal quasi-families, with membership characterized by common symptomatology."[21] The dominant women in

19 *Ibid.*, p. 31.
20 *Ibid.*, p. 33.
21 *Ibid.*, p. 30.

each family tended to feed, protect, and set norms for the group. The members' relationships to the female head seemed stronger than to each other. Shapiro identified five such families containing five to fifteen members each. Three of these families consisted of alcoholics, one of addicts, and one was mixed. The "mentals" were protected fringe members of each of these groups.

Thus the membership composition of the social structure of the rooming house can be seen at two levels to involve the segregating of individuals by common symptomatology. In terms of the neighborhood, social deviants were grouped together in contrast to nondeviants; and within the deviant building different types of deviants were clustered together in social groups. It is interesting to note, however, that in none of these internal groups were the members physically proximate. They usually met together in one another's rooms but were not assigned adjacent rooms. The internal segregating was apparently less important than the external segregating.

However structural change had another aspect, that of change in statuses. All of the occupants suffered from an undesirable status in the eyes of the outside community. Grouping them together in a common "community of the alone" served to isolate and protect them from that status degradation, and permitted them to develop a status system of their own based on acceptance of their behavior. The impact of such an arrangement is significant. For example, the "mentals" were tolerated and cared for in a way that probably could never be achieved in the nondeviant community.

In this sense, the "community of the alone" is a classic example of a source of social change identified by Parsons, the formation of a deviant subcultural movement or group. However, unlike Parsons, who implied that such a development would result in the dissolution of the larger system by negating its basic values, the community of the alone can be seen as a way of achieving many of those basic values of the inclusive system. By accepting the limitations and handicaps which the residents of the rooming house had, it is conceivable that this deviant subcommunity was better able to care for illness and dependency than would have been the case were its members treated under the more repressive conditions of the larger system.

And lastly, structural change involved changes in the composition of the role structure of the rooming house as a neighborhood. In addition to the role of friend and supporter common among neighbors, the roles of family members and of caretaker professionals were added. The effect was to enable the inhabitants of the rooming house to function very much as a self-contained community.

Tools of intervention   Several tools of intervention are demonstrated in this case. It must be recognized that the major structural intervention actually occurred prior to the entrance of the social worker onto the scene, namely the clustering of social deviants into a common residence. This was made possible by virtue of the licensing of single-room occupancy buildings by the City of New York. Thus, public policy to encourage the development of such housing expressed through laws and administrative procedures for licensing and monitoring these buildings is one tool of intervention.

The welfare department was another important factor. Seventy-one percent of the tenants were welfare recipients. Without financial subsidy, such housing would not be available and the group could not have supported itself.

A third important factor was residential stabilization of the population. In order for a system of social relationships to develop there must be some residential stability among the population. If public agencies are constantly harassing or relocating the occupants of single-occupancy rooming houses, such stability is impossible. Relocation is precipitated either by urban renewal projects, or by the funding source, in this case the welfare department. Therefore urban renewal policies and welfare policies that will serve to stabilize the populations of rooming house districts of central cities are necessary ingredients.

A fourth important element was the management of the building. The manager was protective of the tenants and tolerant of their illegal acts. Without such management, it is doubtful that a system of social relationships could develop.

And lastly, the services of a professional caretaker was provided to residents of the building. Whether or not such service is essential is a moot question. In this case the service was supportive of the structural change that had taken place. In the event of a high degree of mobility among leaders of the group who "make it" in terms of the larger society, there may well be a need for a service worker to sustain the group during periods of transition in leadership. In addition, the presence of a sympathetic representative of the "outside" provides a liaison with community agencies for those individuals who wish to obtain treatment for their illnesses, and provides support and assistance for those who wish to migrate out of the system into the larger society.

Residual alternatives   The residual alternatives to such an approach are well known and have a long history. Attempts to save, rehabilitate, and detoxicate the inhabitants of skid row have a long tradition in the field of social welfare. In addition, urban renewal programs in almost every major city have tried to eliminate skid rows by destroying their physical base and dispersing their population. Still a third alternative has been the institutionalization of members of skid row, either through forceful incarceration, or through "hospitalization." Yet, in spite of these efforts, skid rows persist in cities all across the nation. Social welfare agencies provide little more than subsidization of their residents. Urban renewal agencies no sooner complete one clearance project than a new skid row pops up in another section of the city. And in some cities members of skid row migrate almost monthly between their home on the row and the city's "drying out farm."

Implications for social policy   The recognition and acceptance of some deviant subcultures is preferable to institutionalization. The kind of life led by the members in this system of social relationships seems far more humane then that prevailing in most of our public institutions for single unattached individuals suffering from alcoholism or mental illness. Deviants have a greater capacity to tolerate each other than do members of the normal society.

This case would presage that organized efforts to foster the development of such systems will reduce the threat that deviants pose for members of the larger society by enabling them to protect themselves and develop their own means of meeting their needs. At the same time such efforts can assist those who wish to migrate out of the system, as well as facilitate the care of those suffering from illness who remain in the system.

Chapter 5

CASE STUDIES IN
SOCIAL-STRUCTURAL CHANGE :
THROUGH CHANGES IN STATUSES

In this chapter we turn to an analysis of cases in which social-structural change consists of changing the distribution of rights and obligations in a system of social relationships.

In Chapter 4, it was pointed out that to separate role changes from status changes is impossible in actual practice, that an alteration in one inevitably involves a change in the other. A distinction is possible only in terms of strategies of intervention. It is possible to initiate structural change by redefining the roles of a given structure or by redistributing the rights and obligations which accompany those roles.

This interrelatedness of structural characteristics should be kept in mind as we analyze the cases in this chapter. In any discussion of the way in which statuses were changed, it is understood that roles were inevitably redefined as a consequence.

U. S. SUPREME COURT: EQUAL EDUCATIONAL OPPORTUNITY

In these days, it is doubtful that any child may reasonably be expected to succeed in life if he is denied the opportunity of an education. Such an opportunity, where the State has undertaken to provide it, is a right which must be made available to all on equal terms.[1]

The rulings of the United States Supreme Court regarding equal educational opportunity in school systems both North and South constitutes perhaps the most dramatic case of social-structural change in recent years. Since the original 1954 decision in *Brown* v. *Board of Education,* affecting essentially Southern school systems, the Federal courts have written a series of decisions enunciating the right of minority group children to equal educational opportunity in the North.

Much of the public debate regarding school desegregation focuses on the fact that racial discrimination in the provision of public education is unconstitutional. Equal educational opportunity is simply a question of social justice. However, much of the argument in the courts has been more sophisticated. Social science theory has been used to demonstrate the effect of segregation on academic performance.

Since our interests in this analysis are in relating status changes to behavioral problems at the individual level, we will focus on this latter issue. What effect does redefinition of the rights of black children have on their academic performance?

Social problem   For most of the country, the social problem in this case is manifested in the alarming gap in performance between children educated in inner-city ghetto schools and children educated in suburban schools. This discrepancy is of critical social importance because the population of such inner-city schools often encompasses disadvantaged minorities—Negroes, Puerto Ricans, Mexican-Americans—that are dependent on educational achievement for absorption into the mainstream of American life. The plight of the inner-city school has become a major public issue. It has been dramatized and documented by such books as *Blackboard Jungle, Slums and Suburbs, Death at an Early Age,* and most recently *The Coleman Report.*[2] For example, in New York City one out of every three pupils is a year or more behind the norm in reading. In Washington, D. C., pupils in four out of five schools perform below national norms. And in the black ghetto, matters are worse. Nearly 85 percent of Harlem school children are more than

1 *Brown* v. *Board of Education,* 347, U.S. 483, 493 (1954).
2 Evan Hunter, *Blackboard Jungle* (New York: Simon and Shuster, Inc., 1954); James B. Conant, *Slums and Suburbs* (New York: McGraw-Hill Book Company, 1961); Jonathan Kozol, *Death at an Early Age* (Boston: Houghton Mifflin Company, 1967); James S. Coleman, *Equality of Educational Opportunity* (Washington, D. C.: U.S. Government Printing Office, 1966).

two years behind the norm in reading.[3] In a society in which education is a primary vehicle for social mobility, how can the distinct disadvantage of the inner-city child be overcome?

Conceptualization of the problem   The original case reversing the separate but equal doctrine, *Brown* v. *Board of Education*, was based on the finding by the Court that segregated education is unequal education. When black children are prohibited from going to school with white children, they are denied an essential learning, how to relate and compete on an equal basis with whites. Segregation as a state policy depresses the aspirations of blacks by convincing them that they are second-class citizens.

In the years following the 1954 *Brown* decision, litigation has focused primarily on racial imbalance.[4] The original interpretation of *Brown* was that the decision affected only officially enforced segregation. However, as was argued in subsequent cases against Northern school districts, equal harm may be done a black child who goes to an all black school whether it is created directly by law or indirectly by residential patterns. Various lower courts have extended the *Brown* decision to imply an obligation to take positive steps to achieve racial balance where alternatives are available to the state, or where there is "compelling justification" for such affirmative actions. Thus, school boards are prohibited from gerrymandering attendance lines, as in the case of New Rochelle, New York, or from rescinding plans which would result in a step backward in desegregation, as in the case of Denver. School boards can be required to take remedial action where neighborhood residential patterns were established by state actions, such as the location of a public housing project in a black ghetto or the segregation of private developments built under racially restrictive covenants before they were voided by the Supreme Court.

In the case of *Hobson* v. *Hansen*,[5] the District Court for the District of Columbia ordered the school board to desegregate its faculty, to abolish optional attendance zones, to abolish ability grouping, and to transport children from overcrowded school districts which were black to underpopulated school districts which were white. In making these rulings, the court utilized the findings of the Coleman Report, arguing that:

---

3 Maurice R. Berube and Marilyn Gittell, eds., *Confrontation at Ocean Hill-Brownsville* (New York: Frederick A. Praeger, Inc., 1969), pp. 3f.

4 R. M. Rader, "Demise of the Neighborhood School Plan," *Cornell Law Review*, 55 (April 1970), pp. 594–610.

5 *Hobson* v. *Hansen*, 269 F. Supp. 401 (D.D.C. 1967).

the scholastic achievement of the disadvantaged child, Negro and white, is strongly related to the racial and socio-economic composition of the student body of his school. A racially and socially integrated school environ-ment increases the scholastic achievement of the disadvantaged child of whatever race.[6]

The U. S. Supreme Court has refused to review these cases, upholding the right of states to take steps to effect racial balance in the schools.

Had efforts to increase the educational opportunity for black children fixed on the issue of racial balance, this case would be a better demon-stration of changing the membership of a system rather than changing the statuses of the system. However, recent efforts have emphasized the latter approach. According to Rousselot:

Until recently, litigation to achieve equal educational opportunity for Negroes in the public schools of the North and West has not focused as much attention on the allocation of educational resources as it has on racial balance. Yet equal educational opportunity may be denied by the ways in which educational resources are allocated.[7]

Rousselot argues that racial balance as a strategy for achieving equality of education is doomed to failure. Racial balance will be a benefit only in small towns and cities where the number of whites and blacks in the school district makes racial balancing possible, and where the geographical area is sufficiently compact to make it feasible. Large metropolitan areas are usually served by multiple school boards, with school system boundaries often conforming to racially segregated resi-dential areas. In heterogeneous systems such as New York or Los Angeles their very size requires monumental busing in order to achieve racial balance.

In the absence of equity in the distribution of educational resources, racial balance may be a hollow victory. For example, in the state of New York the school district with the highest rank in expenditures per pupil spends seven times the amount of the district with the lowest expenditures per pupil. "Such inequities, which characterize every state in the union, mean the quality of a youngster's education will depend largely upon the place of his birth or residence, matters over which he

---

6 James Bolner, "Legislative Problems Surrounding Racially Balanced Public Schools: A Critical Examination of the Responses and the Prospects," *Vanderbilt Law Review,* 22 (November 1969), p. 1257.

7 Peter F. Rousselot, "Achieving Equal Educational Opportunity for Negroes in the Public Schools of the North and West: The Emerging Role for Private Constitutional Litigation," *The George Washington Law Review,* 35 (May 1967), p. 698.

has no control."[8] Since the property tax is the base for school budgets, the amount of revenue raised is based more on wealth than on need. State aid, when it is based on the amount expended, works to increase such inequities. "Thus, in seven of twelve major metropolitan areas, states now are contributing more per pupil to the suburban schools than to those in the city."[9]

John E. Coons et al., propose a "power equalizing" method of providing state aid by which the gross variations in per pupil expenditures among school districts could be eliminated without negating the initiative of local communities to plan for themselves.[10]

The method would eliminate wealth in terms of a given district's tax base as a factor in determining educational expenditures. Each district would be allowed a standard expenditure depending upon the rate at which it taxed itself. For example, all school districts that taxed themselves at 20 mills would be permitted by state law the same per pupil expenditure, whether they were wealthy districts or poor districts. The excess raised by wealthy districts because of their higher tax base would be taken by the state, and subventions would be given to poorer districts whose tax base would yield substandard funds. The effect of this plan would be to equalize the ability of districts to raise educational expenditures, in relation to the rate at which they were willing to tax themselves.

Like Rousselot, Coons et al., believe that an attack on the present financial structure of education could be made by means of the equal protection clause of the Fourteenth Amendment. In fact, they argue that attempts to achieve such changes through legislation are futile. Intervention by the courts is necessary when individuals seeking protection are of a class that are effectively underrepresented in the political process.

> The testimony of seventy years of frustration of legislative reform strongly suggests the futility of political commotion at the state level where to envoke the democratic process is to ask privileged society to surrender the advantage that as much as any other is the keystone of its privilege.[11]

Attacking the maldistribution of educational resources constitutes a redistribution of rights and obligations. But this redistribution is among systems rather than individuals. As such, it is an example of change in a macro-structure rather than a micro-structure.

8 Ibid., p. 718.
9 Ibid., pp. 718f.
10 John E. Coons, William H. Clune, III, and Stephen D. Sugarman, "Educational Opportunity: A Workable Constitutional Test for State Financial Structures," California Law Review, 57 (April 1969), 305–421.
11 Coons et al., "Educational Opportunity," p. 325.

A more pertinent example of the latter, is the movement to achieve "community control" of the schools.

The rationale behind turning control of inner-city schools over to the residents of the neighborhood in which they are located is conveyed by Jonathan Kozol in the account of his teaching experience in such a school.[12] His book, subtitled "The Destruction of the Hearts and Minds of Negro Children in the Boston Public Schools," attributes the performance of black children in ghetto schools run by middle-class white professionals to the fact that they are judged inferior by middle-class, white standards. According to Kozol's argument, the education of such children is handicapped not so much by individual ability, or the resources spent on their education, as much as by their inferior status in the system.

This phenomenon is exemplified by the Art Teacher who overshadows Kozol's classroom. Her art lesson consists of having black children copy drawings done previously by white students, taking as their subject matter experiences foreign to the blacks.

None of the new drawings, the Art Teacher would tell me frequently, was comparable to the work that had been done in former times, but at least the children in the class could try to copy good examples.[13]

More overt expressions of degradation are reflected in the following passage.

Many people in Boston are surprised, even to this day, to be told that children are beaten with thin bamboo whips within the cellars of our public schools and that they are whipped at times for no greater offense than for failing to show respect to the very same teachers who have been describing them as niggers.[14]

Parents of lower class, black, Puerto Rican, and Mexican children confined to such schools have become increasingly angry in many metropolitan centers around the country. They have agitated to gain control over the selection of personnel who will teach their children, as well as some influence over curriculum, so that this subtle process of degradation can be ended.

This movement had its most dramatic impact in New York City where backers of community control agitated and campaigned for ten

12 Kozol, *Death at an Early Age.*
13 *Ibid.*, p. 3.
14 *Ibid.*, p. 9.

years.[15] It reached a critical point in 1966 when a group of East Harlem parents boycotted Intermediate School 201 demanding the removal of a white principal and the institution of black history and literature courses. In 1967, the New York City Board of Education decided to experiment with decentralization and community control in three districts. Intermediate School 201, Two Bridges, and Ocean Hill-Brownsville.

In implementing this demonstration, the Board appointed principals to three elementary schools within the Ocean Hill-Brownsville demonstration area who had been selected by the local community board established for that purpose. These appointments were made without conformity to the professional requirements of the City or the eligibility lists established by the Civil Service Law. The Council of Supervisory Associations of the Public Schools of New York City filed a suit against the Board of Education and the court ruled that the Board had in fact violated state law.

It appeared that community control was dead. The central issue for which parents fought, the right to control the appointment of school personnel, had been denied them by the court. However, in rendering its ruling, the court recognized the legitimacy of community control,

> ...that in certain communities, specifically disadvantaged areas, the performance of pupils in those schools was far below the level of pupils in other communities and that there was a definite correlation between the schools' performance and parents' involvement in the subject schools.[16]

Convinced of the need for some degree of decentralization, the New York State Legislature in 1967 requested Mayor Lindsey to submit a plan for decentralizing the city school system. The Mayor's proposal, called the Bundy Plan, was opposed by the United Federation of Teachers and the Board of Education as being too decentralized, and it failed in the Legislature. Subsequently, in 1969, the Legislature requested the New York City Board of Education to submit its own plan. The resulting plan called for twenty-nine school districts each with its own board. The district boards would have control over the assignment and transfer of teachers, planning of the curriculum, and selection of textbooks. Educational standards and minimum curriculum requirements would remain the prerogatives of the central board. Following the Ocean

15 Barry D. Hovis, "New York City School Desegregation," *Prospectus,* 3 (December 1969), 228–37.

16 Michael Flynn, "Community Control of the Public School—Practical Approach for Achieving Equal Educational Opportunity: a Socio-legal Perspective," *Suffolk University Law Review,* 3 (Spring 1969), 321.

Hill-Brownsville controversy, the Legislature felt the Board of Education plan went too far and a diluted version of the plan was passed as the 1969 New York Education Act.

The political compromises that resulted in the 1969 Act led Hovis to conclude that administrative decentralization and community control are more apparent than real.[17] While granting to locally elected district boards the right to hire a community superintendent, to appoint teachers, and to select instructional materials, all decisions taken by such boards are subject to approval by the city board. In fact, the city board was granted the right to withdraw powers given to community boards and the right to suspend such boards or individual members.

The tenuousness of community control under such legislation was demonstrated in *Ocean Hill-Brownsville Governing Board* v. *Board of Education*.[18] When the local administrator of the Ocean Hill-Brownsville District removed a number of teachers under the demonstration provisions of the 1968 law, the Board of Education ordered the teachers reinstated. The District refused and the Board suspended the local governing board for thirty days. The members of the local board petitioned the court to terminate this suspension and restrain the Board of Education from interferring in local decision making. The court upheld the actions of the Board of Education as being within the explicit language of the prevailing legislation.

This precedent led Flynn to conclude that community control cannot be achieved through the legislative process. He advocates an alternative strategy based on judicial review of constitutional rights.[19]

Flynn believes there are two constitutional bases for community control: (1) centralization of educational authority causes or preserves inequality of education in ghetto schools, a violation of the equal protection clause of the Fourteenth Amendment, and (2) centralization of educational authority in a pluralistic society constitutes a violation of the Fourteenth Amendment's due process clause.

With regard to the latter issue, he sights a series of attempts by the courts to delineate the right of parents to educate their children free of undue state control.

1. *Meyer* v. *Nebraska*.[20]—The Supreme Court struck down a state statute which forbade the teaching of a modern foreign language to any child under 12 on the basis that it interfered with the freedom of parents to direct the upbringing of their children.

17 Hovis, "New York City School Decentralization," p. 236.
18 294 N.Y.S. 2d 134 (1968).
19 Flynn, "Community Control," pp. 325–40.
20 262 U.S. 390 (1923).

2. *Pierce* v. *Society of Sisters.*[21]—The Supreme Court nullified an Oregon state law requiring children between the ages of eight and sixteen to go to a public school arguing that the constitution "excludes the power of the state to standardize its children."

3. *The Amish and Compulsory Education.*—The continuing resistance of the Old Order of the Amish to compulsory education beyond the eighth grade on the basis that it would destroy their way of life represents a classic precedent. The various court rulings have been ambivalent, marking a continuing effort to find a balance between the state's valid interest in compulsory education and "a countervailing though largely undefined policy of pluralism and deference to minority ethnic groups. . . ."[22]

Flynn justifies control by the black community of the political, economic, and educational structures that govern the operations of local schools as essential to achieving a change in self-esteem. "A long history of oppression has profoundly effected Negro self-esteem."[23] Academic achievement by disadvantaged minorities, he argues, is hindered by low self-esteem, and this can be overcome by changing their rights to self-determination.

Social structure   This series of court cases dealing with equal educational opportunity places the academic achievement of minority group children in the context of the social system of the school. The performance of ghetto children is seen not simply as a result of their individual ability or the quantity of educational resources available to them, but as a function of the social system prevailing in the school.

The system of social relationships on which this analysis focuses is defined in two different ways. In the earlier court decisions it had to do with the relationship between black and white students in a given school. In the latter cases it was defined in terms of the relationship between students, parents, and the administration of the school.

The aspect of this structure undergoing change is the status ascribed to black students. In terms of segregation it is argued that their low achievement results from their perception of themselves as second-class citizens since they are prohibited from attending school with white children. In the case of inner-city schools, poor academic performance was attributed to the inability of minority group parents to influence the administration of their children's education. Community control con-

21 268 U.S. 510, 535 (1925).
22 Note, "The Right Not to be Modern Men: The Amish and Compulsory Education," 53 *Virginia Law Review* 925 (1967).
23 Flynn, "Community Control," p. 340.

stitutes a change in the right of such parents to determine the personnel who will teach their children and to have a voice in determining the subjects which will be taught, prerogatives which are more freely exercised in more homogeneous, suburban communities. This strategy rests on the assumption that once these rights are granted, the self-image of minority group children will be enhanced and their performance improved.

The presumed effect of an increase in the control of schools by parents of disadvantaged, minority group students can be represented graphically (Figure 9). The assumption in this prediction is that white students, or those who are part of the dominant culture, would function at relatively higher levels, even with minimal parental involvement in the schools. The impact would be greater on minority ethnic group members who are politically underrepresented in the dominant institutions of the larger community.

FIGURE 9:
Effect of increase in parental control on academic
performance.

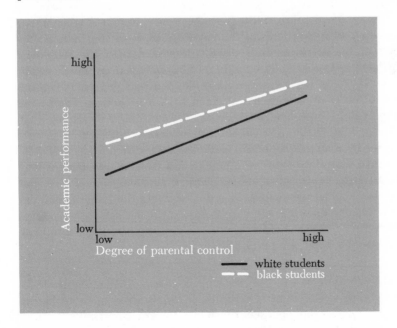

Tools of intervention   The principal means of achieving change in this particular case was litigation or judicial review. There are several grounds on which conflicts of interest are justiciable in our society: (1) When a question exists about the facts of the issue, (2) when administrative policy is unfair or exceeds legal authority, (3) when the intent of legislation is unclear, or when no pertinent legislation has been enacted, or (4) when constitutional requirements are at stake. It is clear from the case of equal educational opportunity that judicial intervention on constitutional grounds is particularly significant in changing statuses.

In most of the conflicts around educational opportunity, legislatures would have been unwilling to rectify the grievances of the parties involved. In fact where legislation was passed, as in the case of the Ocean Hill-Brownsville School District, it tended to work to the detriment of the plaintiffs involved. As one author put it, no majority is about to legislate away its prerogatives. It is for this reason that judicial review is so important as a means of changing the statuses of minority groups in a society which is politically dominated by a permanent majority.

A second major tool of intervention illustrated by the Ocean Hill-Brownsville case is that of organized protest. In essence, the recent efforts to achieve community control have constituted a social movement. Such movements emerge when the issue at hand involves a redistribution of resources which are resisted by those in power, and when those seeking change lack political instrumentalities for exerting influence.

Neither of these two tools is usually identified with the role of a planner. Planners traditionally operate within organizations which establish their own policy. However, certain of the planner's goals may involve the policy of other organizations to which he has no access. The literature on planning is replete with illustrations of the frustrations that result. Under these circumstances judicial review constitutes an important tool, for by a court's ruling on a critical case, external legislative or administrative restraints may be eliminated. Likewise, planners would be well advised to consider efforts which encourage or foster the development of social movements in order to create the kind of political pressure necessary to bring about a readjustment of established policy. The actions of "Nader's Raiders" with respect to consumer problems would represent a typical case in point.

Residual alternatives   The conflict involved in the Ocean Hill-Brownsville case revolves around the issue of professional or technical competence. Those who opposed the move toward community control were largely middle-class professionals who argued that decentralization would reduce the professional or technical quality of education. Theirs was a single standard by which achievement could be explained. It was essentially based on the individual's intellectual skills, the only remedy for which was to increase the technical competence of his instruction.

The argument for community control rests on an alternative assumption. In the absence of any status changes, increased investments in technical education are meaningless. This does not rule out the need for special educational services, but only as a supplement to status change rather than as a substitute.

Implications for social policy   The proposal for community control of vital public services, whether they be education or police protection, has a strong appeal among those concerned about the social problems of large cities.[24] Such an approach as a uniform policy is usually countered by the argument that community control would further isolate poor neighborhoods from any redistributive effect in the allocation of public expenditures. It would seem that this fear could be allayed through attacking the financial structure of state aid to local school districts as proposed by Coons et al.

A more difficult criticism to handle is the question of who speaks for the community. When the service districts involved represent reasonably distinct and homogeneous minority groups which are unrepresented in the political process, community control makes sense. When, however, such districts are heterogeneous, there is no indication that locally controlled schools will be more responsive to their diverse constituencies than those controlled by a metropolitan authority.

The community control proposal must also deal with the issue of insularity. Indeed, it could be argued that the insensitivity of the Boston school system toward blacks was a result of traditions based on the relative homogeneity of dominant ethnic groups throughout large sections of the system.

COLEMAN: COMMUNITY CONFLICT

The monograph by James S. Coleman on the subject of community conflict represents an attempt at hypothesis formulation rather than testing.[25] However, it provides a clear example of a social-structural effect that has implications for social planning.

24 The ultimate extension of this idea is conveyed in Milton Kotler, *Neighborhood Government* (Indianapolis, Ind.: The Bobbs-Merrill Co., Inc., 1969).
25 James S. Coleman, *Community Conflict* (New York: The Free Press, 1957).

Social problem   Coleman's analysis is concerned with the considerable incidence of raw and disruptive conflicts in relatively small communities, usually suburbs or small towns, which rend established social institutions and threaten permanently to divide the community. These incidents have most frequently centered around such issues as fluoridation of the water supply, communism in the schools, and establishment of mental health facilities. While Coleman's analysis covers a wide range of issues related to the origin and course of such conflicts, only one aspect of that discussion—the role of formal organizations in mitigating the disruptive effects of controversy—will be discussed here.

Conceptualization of the problem   Coleman notes that the extent of one's identification with the community will determine the degree to which he participates in disruptive forms of behavior in the course of a community controversy. Those who strongly identify with the community will tend to place preservation of the community above victory for a particular side in a controversy. Such persons are more likely to modify their position, or look for compromises. In contrast, those whose identification with the community is weak will take the stance of the dogmatist or crusader, regardless of its cost to community integration.

Coleman further reasons that identification with the community is mediated in large part through membership in a community-based voluntary organization, such as a church, union, lodge, service club, business, or civic improvement association. It is primarily the uninvolved segment of the community, individuals who are outside the large voluntary organizations, who are most susceptible to participation in disruptive forms of behavior in the course of community conflict.

There is a close analogy between the situations being analyzed by Coleman and the riots in black ghettoes of cities as analyzed by Coser.[26] Coser's analysis adds another dimension to the meaning of membership in voluntary organizations for the course of community conflict. It is not just that such organizations foster a sense of identification with the community; they also serve as powerful lobbying forces securing special benefits for members, differential treatment in the distribution of goods and services. Members are therefore more likely to feel that the system is working in their best interests.

In any event, the Coleman hypothesis would indicate that in communities with a high rate of membership in local voluntary organizations, the probability of violent or disruptive behavior in the course of community conflict is less.

26 Lewis A. Coser, *Continuities in the Study of Social Conflict* (New York: The Free Press, 1967).

For this relationship truly to represent a compositional effect, however, it must be demonstrated that such a "cooling" effect was present among nonmembers as well as members. While Coleman does not explicitly carry his hypothesis to this extent, it seems a logical conclusion. In communities where a majority of residents are participants in the system, there would be less likelihood that nonparticipants would encounter other nonparticipants in sufficiently large numbers to produce incidents, less likelihood of inflammatory incidents or statements reported in the mass media to serve as contagion. Figure 10 indicates the course of the respective curves if this hypothesis were born out in fact.

There is another aspect to the function of voluntary organizations in mitigating community conflicts. Coleman argues that it is not just the density of membership in such organizations, but the interlocking nature of such membership which is important. Communities in which the population is divided into mutually exclusive organizations can have

FIGURE 10:
Effect of level of community involvement in formal
voluntary organizations on participation in disruptive acts.

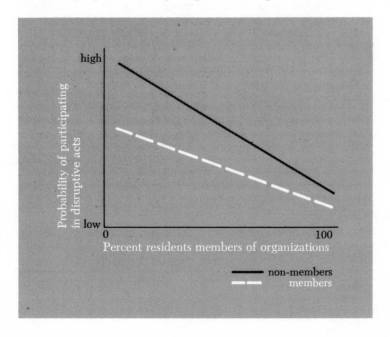

severely disruptive conflicts. One only has to look at the early history of labor unions in this country for an example of this phenomenon.[27]

The overlapping nature of memberships create crosspressures of identification on the individual. Thus, in any given controversy, persons are just as likely to share membership in a given voluntary organization with opponents as will allies on the issue involved. Such crosspressures tend to prevent conflicts from generating personal hatreds among members of opposing sides, which Coleman finds to be the crucial difference between self-contained disagreement and disruptive conflict. A person with multiple identifications has multiple loyalties. This theory of group affiliations has been amply developed by George Simmel.[28]

Following the line of reasoning developed above, it would be possible to predict a compositional effect from the degree of interlocking memberships in voluntary organizations in a given community. In this case, one might plot the behavior not only of individuals with interlocking memberships, but also of members of exclusive organizations, as well as nonmembers of any organization. Their behavior might appear as graphed in Figure 11.

Social structure   Coleman's conceptualization of community conflict deals with the social structure of the decision-making system that exists among the citizens of a local community. The structural aspect dealt with is the position of individuals in that system. Former cases have dealt with characteristics of individuals who occupy positions in a system. In this case, the subject of analysis is the position itself, the statuses of the system.

Position here refers to the membership of the individual in a voluntary formal organization. The number of statuses are two: either member or nonmember. The effect of this membership is to enhance identification or to increase power and influence. Whichever implication is assumed, the reference is the same, the position of individuals with respect to the system.

Structural change, therefore, must involve change in the distribution of these statuses. Thus the objective of intervention is to incorporate all citizens into the network of voluntary formal organizations in the community. The effect is to abolish the status of nonmember, or to equalize the position of influence of all citizens.

---

27 An excellent example is the effect of church membership on the course of a labor dispute in a Southern mill town. See Liston Pope, *Millhands and Preachers* (New Haven, Conn.: Yale University Press, 1942).

28 George Simmel, *Conflict and The Web of Group-Affiliations*, trans. Kurt H. Wolff and Reinhard Bendix (New York: The Free Press, 1955).

FIGURE 11:
Effect of interlocking memberships in voluntary
organizations on participation in disruptive acts.

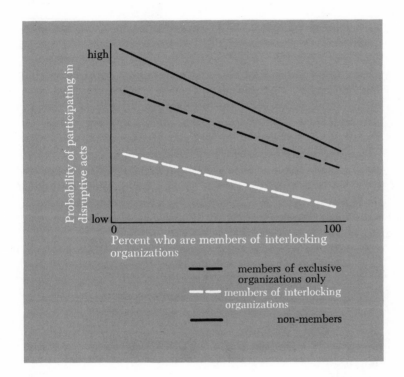

When individuals hold memberships in more than one such organization, their status within the decision-making system of the community
is complicated. They experience a conflicting set of loyalties of rights
and obligations, emanating from membership in different organizations.

To achieve this structural effect, the focus of change is the extent to
which organizations in the community have overlapping memberships.
The effect of overlapping memberships is to create interlocking reference
groups for the individuals involved.

Merton has discussed the concept of reference group as essentially a
group with which an individual identifies for purposes of regulating his
behavior.[29] The structure of interlocking reference groups based on

29 Merton, *Social Theory and Social Structure*, pp. 336ff.

overlapping memberships among formal organizations is illustrated in Figure 12.

FIGURE 12:
Schematic representation of overlapping membership
in formal organizations as reference groups.

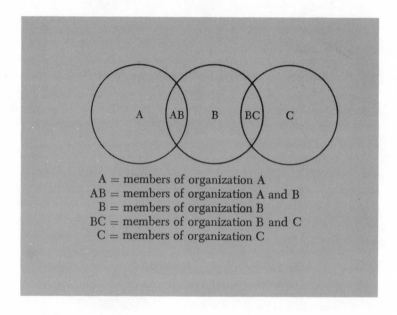

A = members of organization A
AB = members of organization A and B
B = members of organization B
BC = members of organization B and C
C = members of organization C

On any given issue, an attempt by members of organization A to take a position in opposition to organization B, will be blocked by members AB because their reference group includes members B as well as members A.

Tool of intervention   The opportunity for intervention into this system of social relationships occurs at the point of membership formation in voluntary organizations. This point of intervention suggests as a tool the service activity called community organizing. In this case, the planner would engage the services of a community organizer to work with local organizations toward the objective of creating memberships with overlapping reference groups.

This, of course, is not far from the actual historical case in terms of community welfare councils. These councils were consciously created by community organizers as intergroup organizations, that is as a mechanism for bringing together representatives from various organized groups within the community.

It is interesting to note, consistent with this analysis, that the greatest criticism of community welfare councils is that they have tended to be moderating and conciliatory forces in the community, rather than initiators of significant changes in social conditions.[30] Thus, though unsuccessful in their manifest function, they perhaps should be considered quite successful in their latent function of helping to foster community integration.

However, the community council movement may not provide the best structure through which to achieve community integration. Preferred would be a community in which the primary organizations themselves, such as service clubs, churches, unions, and neighborhood organizations had overlapping memberships. The community council is not an organization with primary membership loyalty. Its function as a reference group would not be as powerful as that of a service club, such as Kiwanis, or a neighborhood organization, such as a tenants' council.

Residual alternatives   An alternative to this kind of structural intervention are efforts to negotiate the issues between parties involved in a conflict. Such a strategy may be interminable in communities that are persistently fragmented into isolated and self-contained groups. Creating structures with overlapping reference groups should do much toward preventing the repeated eruption of conflict on issues faced by such communities. The inadequacy of a strategy of negotiation was recognized in the early phase of the civil rights movement, particularly in the South, in which interracial groups were established to provide a vehicle for the two races to get to know each other to create two-way channels of communication, and to prevent outbreaks of racial violence.

Implications for social policy   There are diverging implications for social policy in this analysis. The Coleman approach can be considered as a strategy for "cooling" conflict situations. In this case it is very much applicable to the current university campus scene in which much thought is being given to the need for structures that involve students, faculty, and the administration in policy making.

30 John E. Tropman, *A Comparative Analysis of Welfare Councils* (unpublished Ph.D. dissertation, University of Michigan, 1967).

On the other hand, the Coleman approach can be seen as a means of thwarting the kind of crystalization of issues through conflict which may be essential to social change. For example, in recent phases of the civil rights movement emphasis has been placed on separatism, the creation of black pressure groups to permit a more militant stand on the part of blacks for changes in the social structure of the inclusive community which may affect whites adversely.

This converse of the Coleman hypothesis is also reflected in Martin Rein's study of the Planned Parenthood Federation.[31] Rein found that organizations which had little local policy-making authority were more effective in agitating for local social change because decision making on their part was not subject to the influence of local community reference groups.

The implications of Coleman's hypotheses pertain to the pattern of voluntary formal organizations in the local community. Community organizing should seek to broaden the membership base of such organizations in communities in which participation runs low or where major social cleavages exist. Such efforts should seek to channel increased levels of participation into single-interest organizations if greater equity in the distribution of resources is sought, and into organizations with multiple-interest groups if the reduction of conflict is to be achieved.

CARPENTER: ABLE-BODIED MEN ON SKID ROW

Our last case deals with the problem of public support for "able-bodied men" who inhabit skid row. It is a rather simple case, and may seem to have little public significance because of the small population involved. But the case illustrates clearly the potential of status changes for solving hitherto intractable social problems. It serves as an ideal subject for this analysis.

Social problem   Although the inhabitants of skid row constitute a group with diverse types of social and economic dependency, the prototype of the "rower" is the able-bodied, middle-aged male, whose only reason for not working (aside from a supposed malingering) is excessive if not chronic alcoholism.

In actual fact, skid rowers constitute a mix of homeless men whose economic destitution stems from three major employment handicaps:

---

31 Martin Rein, *An Organizational Analysis of a National Agency's Local Affiliates in their Community Contexts: A Study of the Planned Parenthood Federation of America* (unpublished Ph.D. dissertation, Brandeis University, 1961). See Chap. I.

physical disabilities, old age, and alcoholism. In a 1963 study of Chicago's skid rows, estimated to be the largest in the country, Donald Bogue found the population to be approximately 12,000 such men.[32] Of that number 33 percent or one-third were chronic alcoholics. Fourteen percent were both alcoholic and disabled, while one percent were too old to work in addition to being excessive drinkers.

Financial support for the economically-destitute, homeless man is a problem in our society. If the man is physically disabled, public assistance provides support under the Aid to the Totally and Partially Disabled Program. If the man is over 65, he qualifies for Old Age Assistance, a benign welfare program.

However, assistance for able-bodied men under the age of 65 who are unemployed and not heads of families is more difficult to obtain. These men are eligible only for General Public Assistance (GPA) under the present welfare system. Such assistance is usually time-limited and dependent on the recipient's subjecting himself to rehabilitation for employment. The assumption is that such persons should be employed, and government policy discourages providing them with financial support.

However, the inhabitants of skid row, for the most part, are unemployable in a social sense, even though they may be physically able-bodied. Therefore, they are chronic applicants for GPA. They are periodically sent to "farms" for "drying-out" or detoxification, put through alcoholic clinics for therapy, and enrolled in job training for vocational rehabilitation.

Conceptualization of the problem   Carpenter undertook a follow-up study of men from San Francisco's skid row who had applied for assistance from the City's Welfare Department and had been given treatment.[33]

In 1957, the San Francisco Welfare Department established a Single Men's Rehabilitation Center as a condition for receiving Indigent Aid (GPA). The purpose of the Center was to deter dependent single men from moving to San Francisco in order to receive public assistance, and to provide rehabilitation for employment and re-entry into society for local homeless indigents. The purpose of Carpenter's study was to compare the effect of various treatment programs in operation at the Center in 1961.

---

32 Donald J. Bogue, *Skid Row in American Cities*, p. 82.
33 Edward Carpenter, "Treatment at a Rehabilitation Center and the Subsequent Adjustment of Chronic Drunkenness Offenders" (unpublished D.S.W. dissertation, University of California, Berkeley, 1964); and private interviews held with the author in July, 1969.

As indicated by experience in most cities, such men are poor rehabilitation risks. They fail to sustain any involvement in treatment, they
make little effort to acquire characteristics of employability—to change
their dress or appearance, or to sustain employment in jobs found for
them. Consequently, after a period of time they are dropped from the
welfare rolls or leave the program voluntarily.

In the course of conducting his research, Carpenter uncovered a
serendipitous finding. Discussions with caseworkers in the Department
revealed that in a substantial number of cases a change in the men's
behavior came about as they reached age 65. Upon turning 65, the men
became eligible for Old Age Assistance (OAS). They began keeping
appointments with their caseworkers, dressing more acceptably, manag-
ing their money better, and controlling their drinking. They were less
likely to be "floaters," that is to be without a steady residence, or to
come into conflict with the law. Under Old Age Assistance willingness
to accept employment is no criterion for eligibility; in fact retirement
from the labor market is a norm in the eyes of society.

Social structure   The point of this case is that the inherent
characteristics of these men as social dependents did not change. As
recipients of OAS they were just as economically dependent as recipients
of GPA. Instead, society changed their status by redistributing their
rights and obligations. Upon reaching age 65, they had a right to public
support without employment. They had a position of respectability
rather than degradation.

The system of social relationships in this case can be thought of as
the clients and caseworkers of the welfare department. In this system
there are two statuses for clients, unacceptable dependency and acceptable dependency. When clients exhibit unacceptable dependency, as in
the case of skid rowers, caseworkers respond as agents of social control
using the threat of withholding financial aid to force conformity to
society's standards. When the clients exhibit acceptable dependency, as
in the case of the aged, caseworkers act as societal caretakers seeking
to make life more pleasant and comfortable for those receiving assistance.

The structural change in this case consisted of changing the status
of skid row men from unacceptable to acceptable dependency. The
hypothetical effect of this change on the ability of skid row men to
control alcoholism is graphed in Figure 13.

In this connection it is necessary to ask what effect this change would
have on other groups of able-bodied men under the age of 65 with
varying degrees of financial independence. Figure 13 shows three curves

FIGURE 13:
Effect of change in right to public assistance on control
of alcoholism among able-bodied men under 65.

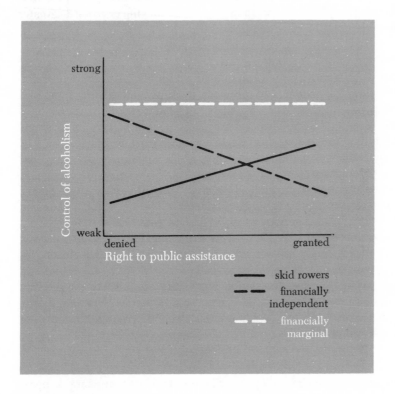

to suggest such possible effects. It is reasonable to assume that a policy change with regard to public support of skid row indigents would have little effect on those who are financially independent when measured by the same criterion, control of alcoholism. On the other hand, there may well be men whose financial security is marginal at best but not insufficient to qualify them for public assistance. A change in public policy providing financial support for skid rowers could affect them adversely, causing a deterioration in their ability to maintain themselves, and literally "driving them to drink." This is, of course, the general problem of disincentives in income maintenance policies.

Although this elaboration of possible effects is hypothetical, it serves as a useful exercise. It reminds the analyst to consider the ramifications of a given policy change on all subgroups of the population, and not just the one on which a desired result can be anticipated.

Tool of intervention   The tool of intervention in this particular case is legislation which governs eligibility for various categories of public assistance. Given the history of public assistance programs, it is more likely that federal programs could be modified toward greater generosity than could state requirements.

Residual alternatives   Containment through incarceration, rehabilitation through mental and physical therapy, and spiritual renewal have been practiced on the "derelicts" of skid row. The results have been discouraging. Recidivism runs as high as 100 arrests for a single man, leading Pittman and Gordon to characterize this practice as *The Revolving Door*.[34] Rehabilitation, whether therapeutic or spiritual, has ended in chronic relapse.

In a recent study by Jacqueline Wiseman, the interaction between the skid row alcoholic and rehabilitation agencies has been documented in one city.[35] Wiseman identifies an underground conveyor system, or what the men call "making the loop." The men play the game of "seeking help" in order to go from one agency to the next to make life on the row a little more comfortable.

According to Wiseman the notion of re-entry into society for the skid row alcoholic is a myth. There are just three ways out: becoming a live-in servant for an institution, entry into an alcoholic rehabilitation profession on the row, or death.

Implications for social policy   The notion of governmental support of able-bodied men young enough to work is an anathema in our society. Yet the alternatives seem ineffective if not inhumane.

According to the findings of Bogue, the burden may not be as large as one would imagine. Of the roughly 4,000 chronic alcoholics on Chicago's skid rows, approximately 2,000 could not be classified as disabled or aged. It may be, that a change of status may render these men more amenable to rehabilitation, and even limited employment.

Outright public support of this segment of the skid row population would have certain benefits. It would reduce expenditures for police, jails, and court services; it would supplant the present system of welfare expenditures both public and private which support the row; and it would obviate the blighting effect which skid rows have on downtown

34 Pittman and Gordon, *The Revolving Door* (New York: The Free Press, 1958).
35 Jacqueline P. Wiseman, *Stations of the Lost* (Englewood Cliffs, N. J.: Prentice-Hall, Inc., 1970).

property values. It may be that the relationships between the costs and benefits of public support would be convincing to a legislature.

In the absence of such evidence, the only avenue for change may be through the courts. As in the case of black children, the men of skid row constitute a minority which is without hope of political representation. If a case can be made for a denial of their constitutional rights, the courts may be convinced to grant relief.

Chapter 6

TOWARD A THEORY OF
SOCIAL-STRUCTURAL CHANGE

INTRODUCTION

Having analyzed cases of social-structural change, it is now possible
to formulate some generalizations about the process of planned intervention to achieve such change.

Throughout this book we have been seeking answers to two basic
questions: (1) How are social problems conceptualized in terms of
social structure? (2) What tools of intervention are available to the
social planner for achieving social-structural change? These questions
reflect the process of planned social-structural change: defining problems
in structural terms, and changing structures to resolve problems. The
conclusions from our case studies should make possible some generalizations about this process. Taken together, these propositions can be
thought of as the basis for a theory of social-structural change.

In making such a claim, we must keep in mind an essential limitation.
The propositions form only a basis for such a theory. The findings from
which they are deduced are in part hypothetical—they have not resulted
from adequate empirical testing. To constitute theory, they must be

formulated in terms of a series of interrelated hypotheses and tested by methods adequate to assure their validity.

CONCEPTUALIZING SOCIAL PROBLEMS IN STRUCTURAL TERMS

We shall attempt to summarize the process used in each of the cases analyzed for conceptualizing social problems in social-structural terms. The extent of commonality among these cases will provide the basis for generalizations regarding the process of reconstructing a given social problem in terms of the structural framework which underlies it. In summarizing we should refer to the basic requisites for the functional analysis of social systems presented by Cancian and discussed in Chapter 2.

In the first place, a social problem must be specified. This usually constitutes a pattern of behavior or condition among individuals which is unacceptable to some segment of society. In terms of a functional analysis, this problematic condition becomes the state, G, of a system of social relationships in which a change is desired. Each of the cases under study had this requisite—racial prejudice, loneliness among the aged, emotional insecurity, crime in the streets, disruptive community conflict, poor academic performance, or social deviancy.

The second step in the process is to identify the system of social relationships in which the problematic behavior takes place. This identification must conform to several criteria. (1) It must refer to a group of actors, that is people who interact with one another. This factor distinguishes a system from an abstract aggregate of individuals who have some characteristic in common but do not necessarily interact, such as the mentally ill, recipients of social security, black people, and so on. (2) It must include all actors or participants involved in the interaction of which the problem is characteristic, not just those who may exhibit the problematic behavior. (3) It must refer to a sustained pattern of interaction, and not an ad hoc one. Obviously instances of sporadic interaction such as crowds or individual acts of violence cannot develop structures or patterns which influence the behavior of the participants. Social systems exist only when there is the expectation of repeated and continued interaction among the persons involved. In the case of Jacobs, the system consisted of the users of a city street, in the Shapiro case it consisted of the residents of a single-room occupancy dwelling, and in the Pearl and Riessman case it consisted of practitioners and clients of a social service agency.

Having specified the state to be changed, and the system of relationships of which that state is characteristic, the next step in the process is to examine the various aspects of the structure of that system which may maintain the behavior in question. It has already been pointed out that there are three aspects of structure which can affect behavior in a system of social relationships:

1. the composition of the population or membership occupying the structure,
2. the composition of the roles in that structure, and
3. the composition of statuses and their relationship to each other.

The first three cases demonstrated that the composition of the membership was a factor which sustained the undesirable state in the system. The next three cases traced this state to role composition. The final three cases related the undesirable state to the composition of statuses.

Lastly, having identified the structural feature which maintains the undesirable state, analysis is made of the alternative means of changing that structural feature which are available to the change agent. These will be discussed as a separate topic in this chapter.

It should be obvious that there are a variety of choices to be made at each step in this process. In part, the range of choices is a function of the extent of knowledge about the problematic behavior in question, but it is also a function of the art of the analyst in being able to imagine alternatives not yet known.

The choice among each range of alternatives will depend on a number of considerations, among them the validity, the desirability, and the practicality of a given alternative. The final conceptualization arrived at will represent an interaction among the choices made at each step along the way. For example, the selection of a particular structural feature for alteration will depend in part on what tools of intervention are available to the change agent.

AN ELABORATION OF STRUCTURAL FEATURES

As indicated by this rather cursory description of the process of social-structural change, there are at least two steps at which the planner is faced with a wide range of choices: identifying relevant structural features of the system of social relationships, and selecting appropriate tools of intervention. The analysis of these cases provides a suggestion of the range of these choices and some idea of the variation among them. An elaboration of this variation will make possible a classification of these phenomena. Such classifications serve a dual purpose: (1) they provide the practitioner with a sort of diagnostic guide to the possible structural interpretations of a given problem, and (2) they provide the measurement devices necessary for further research into the nature of social-structural change.

In elaborating aspects of social structure suggested by the cases under study, a comparison will be made between the types of structural features portrayed in these cases and the range of types conceivable on the basis of our definition of social structure. Where gaps occur in the match between cases and logic, we can extend our model by deduction.

Composition of membership   The cases analyzed portray the use of four different types of membership characteristics as a basis of change in the structure of a system of social relationships. These types are:

1. race
2. age
3. ethnicity
4. social deviancy

As the basis of population groupings, they represent the characteristics of individuals which have a significant impact on social interaction. Their impact arises either from sources inherent in the individual—physiological or psychological states such as age, or from sources inherent in the culture of the individual—evaluations of desirability such as ethnicity or deviancy.

These two types represent a logically complete set of population groupings, although they do not exhaust the variations within such groupings. For example, sex and marital status immediately come to mind as additional types of individually derived influences on social interaction. Examples of characteristics representing social definitions of desirability are practically limitless—education, occupation, income, and residence.

In general, the first group of characteristics is quite close to the basic set of variables studied by demographers. This approximation suggests that demographic characteristics be used as one category for analyzing the effects of membership composition on a system of social relationships.

The second group refers to culturally prescribed values and norms. It suggests that normative characteristics be used as a second category for analyzing the effects of membership composition on such systems.

Composition of roles   The role most frequently identified in the cases under study was that which exists among neighbors, the role of quasi-friend or one who provides mutual support. In the Shapiro case, this neighboring role typical among people sharing adjacent dwellings was augmented by quasi-family roles, the "mother" in subgroups with common symptomatology, and the "children" filled by the mentally retarded. The neighboring role was also augmented by quasi-social service roles, that of the "visiting nurse," the "homemaker," and the "therapist" dispensing tranquilizers.

In the Jacobs case, the predominant role enacted on the city street, that of the "stranger" who comes only to buy or sell a given good or service, was augmented by the role of the "proprietor," one who feels a certain sense of ownership of the city street and who seeks to protect it.

The Pearl and Riessman case focused on the composition of work roles of a social service agency. They were augmented by the role of the expediter, one who negotiates agreements between practitioners and clients.

The common characteristic of these roles seems to lie in their fulfilling some basic human need common to members of the system of social relationships: mutual support, nurture, provision of food and shelter, care of the sick and dependent, distribution of goods and services, and protection or social control. In this sense roles can be thought of as performing functions for the system of social relationships.[1] What is needed, therefore, is a classification of such functions which might be used to test the adequacy of this elaboration of types of roles.

Warren provides one such classification with reference to the local community as a social system which seems particularly relevant to the purposes of this analysis.[2] He posits five such functions: production-distribution-consumption, socialization, social control, social participation, and mutual support. Our cases illustrate roles which foster mutual support, social control, and, to a limited degree, production-distribution-consumption. Conspicuous by their absence are roles fostering socialization such as "teacher" and roles fostering social participation such as "leader." These latter roles are more prevalent in formal organizations such as the school, factory, and club.

Composition of statuses   On the basis of our theoretical framework, the composition of statuses or the distribution of rights and obligations within a system of social relationships can be conceptualized in two ways—as hierarchical or lateral. The cases analyzed contain examples of both types.

---

1 This observation has been made by Parsons. "There is the same order of relationship between roles and functions relative to the system in social systems, as there is between organs and functions in the organism." *The Social System*, p. 115.

2 Roland Warren, *The Community in America*, Chap. 6.

Many of the cases implied a hierarchical stratification in terms of the statuses ascribed to majority and minority groups in our society, to social conformers and deviants, or to positions in a work organization. The cases involving systems of relationships among neighbors and quasi-families or among students in a classroom contained essentially lateral statuses in which a division of labor or equality of treatment was the basis of arrangement.

Although this abstract dichotomy logically exhausts the types of status arrangements, it obviously can be thought of as the polar extremes of the continuum with an indefinite number of variations in between. For example, one can think of student statuses as equal. Yet on the basis of interest and ability in relation to a given subject matter some students will be treated "more equally than others" in the distribution of a teacher's time. Likewise, in relation to a service agency, the entrance of the expediter tends to equalize the distribution of rights and obligations between the client and practitioner, but not as much as if the service were being purchased by the client on the open, competitive market.

AN ELABORATION OF TOOLS OF INTERVENTION

We come now to the second basic question of this analysis, namely, what are the tools available to the planner for accomplishing social-structural change?

In recapitulating the tools identified in each of the cases studied, there emerges a varied list.

1. In the Deutsch and Collins case the tool was the tenant selection policies of a public, statutory agency.
2. In the Rosow case, the tools were tenant selection policies of private and public property owners and financial incentives from the government for housing construction.
3. In the Rosenberg case, the tools were the construction and location of community facilities, and community control of public services.
4. In the Jacobs case, the tool was land use controls.
5. In the Pearl and Riessman case, the tool was administrative reorganization.
6. In the Shapiro case, the tools were licensing of single room occupancy dwellings, public rent subsidies, and tolerance in the application of public law with respect to deviant populations.
7. In the case of equal educational opportunity, the tools were litigating the constitutionality of state actions, and organized protests.
8. In the Coleman case, the tool was community organizing.
9. In the Carpenter case, the tool was legislation.

An examination of this array of intervention tools reveals several areas of commonality. By so classifying them, the original list appears to consist of special cases of more general purpose tools.

1. Land use controls, licensing, and eligibility requirements for public assistance are all special cases of *legislation*.
2. The location of community facilities, tenant selection policies, the policing of deviants, and the reassignment of functions within a service agency are matters usually regulated by the *administrative policies* of formal organizations, even though they may be bounded by law.
3. Financial incentives for construction and rent subsidies are example of *public expenditures*, which are determined through budgetary processes even though enabled by law.
4. Community organizing and citizen protests are manifestations of the use of *political power* for creating sanctions for change outside of legally established authority.
5. Litigation of state actions is a form of *judicial review*.

It should be recognized that these general classes are not mutually exclusive, that they are to some extent overlapping. However, they emphasize distinctly different methods of achieving change. Each of the specific tools identified within this study can be located logically within one of these five general classes. Because of the lack of exclusiveness among the general classes, the special cases could be assigned to more than one category. For our purposes, it is enough to show that they can be assigned to at least one.

The adequacy of this elaboration of general classes of intervention tools can be tested by reference to a typology developed by Lindblom.[3] Lindblom identifies four basic ways in which policy is formulated: (1) by administrative regulation, (2) by legislation, (3) by judicial review, and (4) by citizen pressure.

If we look at the tools of intervention identified in these cases, we find that most of them fall under administrative regulation and legislation. Public expenditures, which represent the combined effect of legislation and administrative regulation, are treated as a separate category because each constitutes an important and distinct planning tool. (See Figure 14.) That our cases fell primarily into these categories is not unreasonable given the traditional context of planning practice. Judicial review was identified in only one of our cases. As an intervention tool judicial review is being relied upon increasingly as advocates of the

3 Charles E. Lindblom, *The Policy-Making Process* (Englewood Cliffs, N. J.: Prentice-Hall, Inc., 1968).

FIGURE 14   *Tools of intervention for social-structural change: Special purpose and general purpose.*

Tools of Intervention	
Special purpose	*General purpose*
land use controls licensing eligibility requirements for public assistance	legislation
location of community facilities tenant selection policies policing of deviants	administrative regulation
financial incentives for construction rent subsidies	public expenditures
community organizing community control of public services	political power
constitutional guarantees of equal treatment and citizen rights	judicial review

poor seek to change the rights of people to receive benefits from health, welfare, and housing programs.

And lastly, Lindblom identifies the role of the citizen as a voter, as a member of organized pressure groups, and as a participant in civil disobedience. In this connection, the whole phenomenon of social movements is relevant. Such efforts are necessary when the changes sought go against the interests of those in power, and when those who seek change do not grant legitimacy to those in power. The current interest in community organization—expressed through the civil rights movement, the welfare rights movement, the peace movement, and the women's liberation movement—is an example of this tool of intervention in social-structural change.

To understand the function of social movements in achieving social-structural change, it is necessary to refer to the relationship between power and legitimacy as discussed by Stinchcombe.[4] The ability to make public policy involves the right to exercise certain powers over other members of the body politic. This right is granted to such policymakers

4 Arthur L. Stinchcombe, *Constructing Social Theories* (New York: Harcourt Brace Jovanovich, Inc., 1968), pp. 158–63.

.rt by those over whom the power is exercised, but also by other
nu..ers of power in society. It is the willingness to back up or support
these rights on the part of subordinates and/or other centers of power
that constitutes the legitimacy of a given set of rights.

Social movements arise when certain groups of citizens, members of
the body politic, no longer recognize the legitimacy of public policymakers or other power holders to exercise their rights. Such movements
are an attempt to redefine and reassign such rights on more acceptable
terms. Hence the labor movement through unionization has succeeded
in redefining the right of management to make decisions regarding
wages and working conditions. Blacks and other minority group members, through the civil rights movement, have succeeded in redefining
the right of government and businessmen to discriminate against their
members. The welfare rights movement is seeking to achieve a new
definition of the rights of welfare departments with respect to the
allocation of welfare benefits. This phenomenon was reflected in our
cases by the movement for community control of the schools on the part
of minority group parents.

It can readily be seen that the effect of such social movements is
to redistribute rights and obligations among various members within a
system of social relationships. This is not to say that social movements
are the only means of achieving such change. As Stinchcombe has
pointed out, other centers of power upon whom a given power holder
depends for legitimacy may force a change in the exercise of rights.
Social movements often play a critical role in exploiting such divisions in
the power structure. In the face of a united front of power holders, they
constitute the only means of achieving status changes.

This discussion of social movements brings us full cycle to an analysis
made in Chapter 1 regarding the concept of structural change in social
work practice. We pointed out that while community organization may
imply the assumption that problems have their roots in the social
environment, it does not always lead to structural solutions. If community organization is to result in social change it must achieve some
redistribution of power which becomes institutionalized, as was the case
with union organizing, and the efforts of black and Puerto Rican parents
in the Ocean Hill-Brownsville community school. The same can be said
of social movements—that they are only a tool of intervention, not an
end in themselves. It is the rearrangement of power which they hope to
institutionalize that constitutes social change.

Since planners have traditionally operated within the established
system of power, legitimated either by administrators or legislators, it
should not be surprising that the traditionally recognized tools of intervention are endogenous to that framework of policy making. This analy-

sis suggests that judicial review and social movements are also relevant for planners as a strategy for intervention in the policy-making process.

IMPLICATIONS FOR SOCIAL POLICY: ADDING UP THE SCORE

Although our primary objective is not to devise public policy prescriptions, one cannot help but notice the findings of the cases reported, and be concerned about their policy implications.

In looking at all nine case studies, the policy implications appear to be contradictory. Some cases, such as the Deutsch and Collins case and the Coleman case, seem to argue for a policy of integration. Other cases such as those of Rosow, Rosenberg, and Shapiro seem to represent arguments in favor of a policy of segregation. Do these cases, in fact, support one policy over another? Is there a built-in predisposition in the model of social-structural change that encourages or precludes homogeneity of population groups?

In a factual sense the contradiction is a false one. As was pointed out earlier, none of the specific studies result in findings that suggest the desirability of either complete homogeneity or heterogeneity. Neither Rosow nor Rosenberg argue that residential neighborhoods should be 100 percent homogeneous. Rosow concludes that a given minority group, in this case the aged, must constitute about 50 percent of the population involved. Rosenberg concurs in the case of religious minorities. The point is, there must be enough members of a given minority group in the immediate environment to provide the basis for a supportive system of social relationships.

Such a policy does not prevent integration, or interaction between members of the minority and majority groups. What it does provide is the freedom of minority group members to mix if they choose, or to stay with their own kind should that be their interest. When a minority group member is isolated from other members of his group he has no choice but to subject himself to relationships with majority group members which may be detrimental. It should be noted that the three cases arguing for some degree of segregation involve subgroups of our society that have been ascribed an inferior social status, members of racial minorities, the elderly, and social deviants.

In another sense this apparent contradiction in policy implications is unreal. The tendency to cast the cases in a segregationist-integrationist mold reflects but one way of reading the cases. It involves a public preoccupation with a specific issue in race relations today. As an alternative one could read pluralism in place of segregation. What the Rosow, Rosenberg, and Shapiro cases suggest is that true acceptance of the interests and behavior of minority groups in our society may best be brought about by the recognition of their right to be different, including the right to have their own system of social relationships and accompanying supportive institutions. In a similar vein, the term integration can mask stability, the tendency to maintain the status quo in a given social system. For what the Deutsch and Collins, Jacobs, and Coleman cases illustrate is how to prevent open conflict between groups in our society which may be at odds with one another on basic issues.

There is another theme which runs through many of the cases, that of equality among positions of a given system. The Shapiro case, the Supreme Court case, and the Carpenter case all seem to argue that complete equality in the distribution of rights and obligations will solve all our problems. Is there no circumstance under which stratification is desirable? Does social change necessarily mean social leveling?

The notion of complete equality in social arrangements is particularly alluring today with the acute awareness of the many injustices built into our present social order. But Parsons warns us not to confuse social revolution with the absence of social stratification. He notes that even revolutionary social movements, if they are to succeed, must overcome their preoccupation with egalitarianism and establish some form of differential rewards.[5] The Quakers operate with a marked degree of equality among their members, but they pay a heavy price in inefficiency.

The point to be made is that social-structural change is not necessarily egalitarian. It is a method by which change in the established patterns of stratification can be measured in relation to the goals of the system, the needs of its members, and the resources at its disposal.

One can only conclude that the implications of these studies are more complicated than a simple dichotomy would suggest. Furthermore, there is no inherent tendency in the model of social-structural change to generate one kind of policy as opposed to another. What these cases illustrate is that different changes in the structure of a system of social relationships can result in differing states. The crux of the matter is to analyze the function that different aspects of the structure have for a given state of the system, and to anticipate the changes that will result from their alteration.

QUESTIONS FOR FURTHER STUDY

In any analysis such as this there are always aspects of the guiding questions that remain unanswered. Since the object of theory is to

5 Talcott Parsons, *The Social System,* p. 526.

provide a comprehensive and internally consistent explanation of the subject under study, such gaps in understanding must be bridged.

It is appropriate, therefore, to examine those aspects of our subject that require further investigation. Some of these questions were recognized at the outset and specifically set aside. They need to be recalled at this time. Additional questions have arisen out of the analysis itself.

Quality of the evidence   One such issue is the validity of the claims regarding the effects of social-structural change presented in the case material analyzed. Having elaborated and defined the concept and its use, it becomes necessary to establish its consequences in fact.

In some of our cases such evidence was presented with some degree of adequacy. However, in other cases the answer to the question—Does social-structural change really affect behavior?—remains in the realm of speculation. For example, in the Jacobs analysis, a clear and reasonable argument was made for the way in which social-structural change might reduce street crime. However, the evidence supporting this claim was selective in order to illustrate the relationship between land use patterns and social interaction on the streets. The author did not rigorously examine the universe of urban neighborhoods to see how consistently the relationship obtained. There is the disturbing possibility that in neighborhoods of intense poverty, where land use mix and social interaction are high, her hypothesis will not hold. Poor neighborhoods ironically often suffer from the worst crime rates.

The same is true of the Shapiro case. The impression that social-structural change with reference to the occupancy of the rooming house reduced threats to the surrounding neighborhood and enhanced the functioning of the residents was clear in the mind of the reporter. However, more objective data about the relative wellbeing of all the residents is needed in order to counteract the tendency to romanticize "life in the slum."

The most critical limitation to the validity of our analysis is the fact that cases were chosen which illustrate that social-structural change can make a difference. For the purposes underlying this book—namely to determine how problems can be conceptualized structurally, and to identify tools of intervenion—this strategy was appropriate. However, if the question—Does it really work?—is to be answered, negative cases must be examined, instances in which social-structural change did occur, but no corresponding change in behavior resulted.

Such an examination is essential, not so much to prove the validity of the general argument, which has been substantiated by those cases in which adequate evidence was available, but rather to make more specific the conditions under which such change has an impact. A more precise picture of the types of situations which can be dealt with through social-structural change and those that are less amenable to this form of intervention could only be demonstrated by negative results in cases where this strategy was inappropriate or inapplicable.

Efficacy of structural change   Another question raised and set aside at the outset of this study is, how much difference does social-structural change make? Granted the validity of behavioral effects, what is the relative impact of social-structural change compared with the change resulting from residual treatments?

This question is clearly raised in the Rosenberg case but never answered. It will be remembered that Rosenberg himself explicitly qualified his findings by saying that a religiously consonant neighborhood context reduced the likelihood of emotional insecurity during adolescence but did not prevent it. There were, Rosenberg hypothesized, other fundamental sources of mental illness outside the social milieu.

Cases should therefore be examined in which social-structural change is contrasted with other types of intervention to determine the relative merits of the former approach in relation to varying conditions and circumstances. For example, the Shapiro case could be replicated under more rigorous experimental conditions, comparing the effect of psychotherapy in the absence of any attempt to build a patient subsystem, with the effect of a housing program, such as "a half-way house," that fosters a sense of group identity among persons with mental illness without the assistance of psychotherapy. Similarly, the Carpenter case lends itself to verification and greater specificity. To what extent does a redefinition of the status of a skid row man under the age of 65, in the form of an automatic pension and a sort of medical discharge from the labor market, result in a reduction in alcoholism in contrast to attempts at medical rehabilitation?

Feasibility of structural change   A third unanswered question is the extent to which social-structural change is feasible in all situations. Obviously there are practical limitations to converting every social problem into social-structural terms.

A very clear example of this limitation is contained in the Jacobs case. One of the most frequent criticisms of her analysis of street crime is that it is feasible only in "old world neighborhoods" such as Greenwich

Village or the North End of Boston; that most sections of modern cities do not have the kinds of population and potential for mixed land use that her analysis requires. Therefore, a very legitimate question is, given the validity of her analysis, how useful is it for solving the problem of street crime on a general basis throughout the urban community?

To answer this question it would be necessary to extend the analysis developed by Jacobs to a variety of types of sections of the urban community to determine its feasibility under varying conditions. A similar extension of the other case examples cited in this study is warranted.

Negative effects   In considering the cases we have presented the reader at some point may have asked the question, is this a desirable change? Social-structural change, to use Cancian's formula, may result in the disappearance of an undesirable state G, but may result in the appearance of another state G that is also undesirable. The negative effects of social-structural change have not been analyzed in this book.

A clear example of this problem is implied in several of the cases involving the grouping of populations with similar belief systems or pathologies. What is at issue here are the negative implications of current proposals for a "ghetto policy." While homogeneous arrangements may have positive effects in relation to the problems we have identified, they may also produce negative effects with respect to other conditions. A classical example is the provincialism that is attributed to the Boston Irish ghetto. Provincialism creates barriers to adaptation on the part of members of an exclusive group to social and technological changes occurring in the inclusive society from which they have set themselves apart, but without which they cannot prosper.

In addition, social-structural change raises the very thorny issue of individual freedom of choice. At the outset it was indicated that one asset of residual treatment is the self-selectivity of the persons affected. In social-structural change, the individual loses his freedom to choose inclusion. His only recourse is to withdraw from the system of social relationships, or to create compensating subsystems.

In spite of the presence of negative effects, either presumed or real, the social planner cannot easily turn away from such intervention. Social-structural change is occurring whether intended or not, whether for social good or private gain. Real estate developments are an obvious case in point. The issue really becomes how best to equip the social planner to deal with this dimension of problem solving so that social objectives may be better served.

Controlling secondary effects   Two additional questions emerge as a result of our analysis. They have to do with controlling the effects of the change of one subsystem on (1) other subsystems, and (2) states within the inclusive system.

It was noted in Chapter 2 that any change in a given subsystem must result in a compensatory change in another subsystem if the inclusive system is to maintain equilibrium. And conversely, when such change cannot be compensated, change of the inclusive system results. This study has ignored these secondary effects. In order to use social-structural change effectively as a method of problem solving it is necessary to know the capacity for compensatory changes in other subsystems, as well as to know whether or not change will occur in the inclusive system.

This interrelatedness of change effects can be illustrated, as in Figure 15. The "target subsystem" refers to the system of primary interest such as the cases we have analyzed. "Related subsystems" refer to any other subsystem in the inclusive system of which the target subsystem is a part. The inclusive system for the cases in this book refers to the local community at large.

Following Cancian's model, the alternatives can be outlined as follows:

1. A change *of* the target subsystem consistent with a state G, in the inclusive system, will not be threatened by compensatory changes in related subsystems (pattern I).
2. A change *of* the target subsystem contrary to a state, G, in the inclusive system, accompanied by a compensatory change *of* related subsystems will result in maintenance *of* the inclusive system with regard to a given state (pattern II). Such a pattern is called "change *within* the system" with respect to the inclusive system.
3. A change *of* the target subsystem contrary to a state, G, in the inclusive system, which results in a sympathetic change *of* related subsystems, i.e. a change in the same direction, will inevitably result in a change *of* the inclusive system with respect to that state (pattern III). Such a pattern will be called a "change *of* the system" with respect to the inclusive system.

These patterns can be illustrated by the cases presented in this book. For example, the Deutsch and Collins case attempts to reduce prejudice by integrating residents of different races in a public housing project. The public housing project can be thought of as a target subsystem with the surrounding neighborhood as a related subsystem within the inclusive system of the urban community.

The response of the related subsystem to what happens in the public housing project can be in either of two directions. On the one hand, if it values the existing pattern of segregation, it can be threatened by

FIGURE 15   *Patterns of interrelatedness in change of subsystems and inclusive systems.*

Patterns	Target Subsystem	Related Subsystems	Inclusive System
I (Deutsch and Collins)	State G: racial segregation Change: racial integration	State G: racial segregation Reaction to change: acquiescence or isolation	State G: racial integration Effect of change: maintenance of system
II (Ocean Hill-Brownsville)	State G: professional control of schools Change: parental control of schools	State G: professional control of schools Reaction to change: retaliation or rejection	State G: centralized control of schools Effect of change: maintenance of system
III (Shapiro)	State G: rejection of deviants Change: tolerance of deviants	State G: rejection of deviants Reaction to change: sympathetic change	State G: rejection of deviants Effect of change: change of system

such a change of the target subsystem and either retaliate with hostile actions or isolate the housing project from neighboring subsystems. On the other hand, if it favors integration, it might accept the change of the target subsystem or even imitate it with changes in its own patterns.

What happens in related subsystems will depend in part on the state of the inclusive system. If the state of the inclusive system with regard to prejudice favors the reduction of prejudice, e.g., community-wide norms that support equality, then changes of related subsystems which would threaten or counteract changes of the target subsystem would most likely be prevented by the inclusive system. Such a relationship is foreseen by Deutsch and Collins when they note that the success of their case depends on supportive attitudes in the wider community.

If, however, the state of the inclusive system supports segregation, then changes of the target subsystem would threaten maintenance of the inclusive system unless related subsystems compensated for it in a negative way, i.e. by isolating the target subsystem or attempting to destroy it.

This contrasting pattern is illustrated by the Ocean Hill-Brownsville case. The academic achievement of minority group children was to be raised by giving their parents control over their local schools. This move on the part of the local community was forcibly opposed by a related subsystem, the teachers union. The union obviously saw in this demonstration a threat to professional control of other units of the school system. The Board of Education, representing a more inclusive system, saw in this a threat to centralized control, and opposed the exercise of unilateral power by the community in running local schools. The state legislature, an even more inclusive system, backed up the Board of Education with legislation that maintained ultimate control with the Board of Education.

Thus an attempt to change a state of the target subsystem, professional control of the schools, was fought by a related subsystem, and effectively prevented by lack of concurrence by the inclusive system.

The Shapiro case illustrates the potential for the third pattern of interrelatedness between subsystems and the inclusive system: change of the inclusive system resulting from sympathetic changes among subsystems.

The segregation of social deviants into quasi-family housing groups can be thought of as a means of meeting the needs of the members involved. When this happens, the nature of their dependency on the larger community changes. They no longer see themselves as "sick," seeking treatment and rehabilitation. Their principal unmet need is for material support. However, such support in our society is provided on the basis of conformity to certain norms (state G of the inclusive system), for example gainful employment and adherence to standards of behavior. The expectation on the part of rooming house tenants to receive goods and services without such conformity is a direct threat to the maintenance of those norms in the larger community.

Social service agencies (related subsystems) customarily provide material support to such populations. It is understandable why considerable public pressure is exerted on these agencies to require recipients to submit to some form of rehabilitation. If social service agencies respond sympathetically to an expectation on the part of deviants of support without conformity, the social norms of the larger community are threatened.

Such appears to be the case with respect to the welfare rights movement which is now demanding money without work in a society which expects work for money. The welfare department, a related subsystem, is caught in the middle; at first it responds sympathetically to the welfare mothers' demands and then being apprised of the danger of such a reaction to the inclusive system, it seems to retrench to a position of rejecting such demands.

Not all of our cases exhibit patterns of interrelatedness with other subsystems and inclusive systems. For example, the kinds of changes involved in the cases by Rosow, Rosenberg, and Jacobs do not appear to depend on reactions of related subsystems or more inclusive systems. This observation supports the notion that structural change does not always have ramifications in related systems. The degree of independence of a given subsystem is an important factor in determining the feasibility of a proposed structural change.

These patterns of interrelatedness among subsystems and between subsystems and the inclusive system must be explored further in order to render social-structural change a more adequate model of social planning.

DEFINING LIMITATIONS

Aside from the limitations of our model as a contribution to social theory, it is important to indicate its limitations with respect to practice. Social-structural change as we have defined it is applicable within a limited set of circumstances. These circumstances can be elaborated in three respects: (1) the scale of change, (2) the power to change, and (3) the sanctions to change.

The scale of change implied in this model of practice involves subsystems of society in contrast to social systems in an inclusive sense. It deals with changes in pieces of the social scene rather than the whole social order. In addition, there is a geographical scale implied. The kinds of changes discussed in this study are those which occur in the local community and which can be achieved through local actions, even though national decisions may be involved. The model of change is also circumscribed by limited powers available to accomplish such change. Underlying this model are powers usually available to local and state government. These powers include control over legislation, public expenditures, taxation, judicial processes, and the administrative policy of major community organizations such as governmental boards, commissions, and voluntary organizations. These powers are certainly real; however, they are not inclusive or massive with respect to the range of forces effecting social change.

In addition, this model rests on the assumption that the planner or change agent is located in a position with respect to these powers that provide him the opportunity for significant influence over their use. For example, the change agent must be located in some direct line of influence over the mayor or governing boards of formal organizations.

And lastly, the question of sanctions or authority must be raised. As has been noted before, social-structural change involves the rights of all members of a given subsystem. The question can be asked, by what authority does the planner or change agent affect these rights?

One answer stems from the fact that some authorities are explicitly delegated to the planner or change agent through such institutions as zoning laws, licensing laws, and organizational budgets. In these cases the planner acts on the basis of some degree of democratically derived sanctions. Nevertheless, even delegated authority requires provision for ongoing citizen review (sometimes called advisory boards), to provide a check on the interpretation of that delegated authority and its possible misuse.

Beyond this range of delegated sanctions, the planner or change agent will have to create authority for changes he desires. In this case the planner may propose change to some decision-making body which presumably represents a degree of democratic control, e.g. the city council or the elected board of a formal organization. Or he may create a constituency and a decision-making procedure which would generate some degree of public sanction for his proposed plan or change.

A danger lies in the fact that it is always possible for the planner or change agent to operate covertly or to effect structural change without explicit sanction. Such is often the case with highway departments which rearrange whole communities and their populations without due citizen approval. Such a mode of operation is not consistent with a democratic philosophy, nor viable in the long run in an open society.

In the last analysis it must be recognized that the model of planning inherent in this study is essentially a reformers' model. It implies initiatives on the part of individuals who see problems in the way the present system works in terms of a given set of values, and who seek to resolve those problems according to some standard of human welfare. The interests of reformers do not always coincide with a majority point of view or a majority definition of the common good. Reformers often propose changes which though sound and reflective of "the greatest good for the greatest number," are appreciated by only a distinct minority. Ultimately proposals for social-structural change must involve some process of accountability to the population affected, otherwise they become the weapon of demagogues or the tools of a totalitarian state. Social-structural change must not be thought of as a self-contained, self-justified model of change, but rather as one analytical input into a process of decision making that ultimately requires political evaluation and adaptations.

Chapter 7
IMPLICATIONS FOR THE SOCIALLY-ORIENTED PROFESSIONS

A NEW DEFINITION OF SOCIAL PLANNING

We now return to the question with which this book began—specifically, how best to attack the social problems currently facing society. The major implication of our analysis leads to a new definition of social planning.

We recall that current attempts to define the nature of social planning originate primarily within those professions that have staked a claim within the area of social problem solving. Such definitions take either of two forms, both of which are inadequate from the point of view maintained here.

The more traditional and most frequently expressed definition is often referred to as *sectorial planning* because it deals with the projected need for money and manpower to meet the demand for services within an established domain of professional practice, i.e. social welfare, education, health. The assumption underlying this definition of planning is that social problems in essence are nothing more than the aggregate of individual problems which would be resolved if only society would allocate enough resources to the professions servicing these pathological categories. Within our framework such a definition has been called a residual approach to social problem solving because the objects of change are the victims of the social order rather than the way in which society is organized. In this sense sectorial planning is an inadequate definition of social planning.

The alternative tendency is to define social planning as *comprehensive planning*. This notion stems from the uneasy realization that social problems persist in spite of the best efforts of existing professions and disciplines to solve them. It rests on the assumption that this elusiveness results from a piecemeal approach rather than a comprehensive approach to planning. If all the present professions and services were integrated into one grand social design, the social problems of our society would be resolved. Comprehensive planning assumes that the frame of reference of the individual professions is sufficient within their domain of practice —all that is lacking is some rational overview.

The naïvete of this approach has already been argued. Planning requires some integrating principle, some overall set of goals and objectives. Obviously no such unity of function or consensus of purpose exists for society in all its aspects. In short, comprehensive planning is an impossibility. Problem states must be specified, specific goals must be selected out of the myriad strivings characteristic of social beings.

The concept of social planning which we advocate is called *social-structural change*. Its underlying assumption is that the source of social problems lies somewhere in the social order, the organized set of relationships which exist among individuals engaged in a system of interaction. It is preferred because it is more natural; it deals with the normal context in which people live and interact and not clinical abstractions. It is more basic in the sense that it gets at more fundamental roots of social problems. It is not reductionist; it does not reduce social problems to characteristics of individuals. It is more realistic in the sense that it affects everyone involved and not just those who take advantage of individualized resources.

SOCIAL-STRUCTURAL CHANGE AS PROFESSIONAL PRACTICE

A very legitimate question can be raised—to what extent can social-structural change be identified as an area of professional practice? Is there a methodology for such change which can be codified and transmitted through some formal training program? Do the tools of intervention identified in this analysis fall within the domain of practice of any of the existing socially-oriented professions? The answer to these questions involves some analysis of what constitutes a profession.

Characteristics of a profession   Wilensky and Lebeaux, in discussing the nature of professionalism, identify two distinctive characteristics of a profession: (1) the possession of exclusive technical competence, and (2) norms of conduct governing professional behavior.[1] It is the former characteristic that is more relevant to our objectives.

Two efforts are involved in establishing exclusive technical competence. On the one hand, professions seek to develop a clearcut body of knowledge, usually scientific in nature, as the basis for practice. Only evidence of the possession of such technology warrants respect by the society for the value of the professional service involved.

Once established, the profession attempts to carve out exclusive domain over this technology through specialized training programs, legal restrictions, and employment practices that prevent nonmembers of the profession from gaining access to this technology. Wilensky and Lebeaux argue that the profession can claim no special status in terms of that if the mastery of this technology is not exclusive, the receipt of respect and resources from society.

Meyerson, in a similar vein, analyzes these characteristics from the standpoint of "the natural history of professionalization."[2] He draws out some problems of professionalism which are particularly relevant to our objectives.

Meyerson's natural history falls into three phases. The *pre-professional phase* is one in which people of "imagination and a profound dissatisfaction with the world as they see it" focus their efforts on identifying new problems and proposing new approaches to their solution. Characteristic of this phase is the focus on problems neglected by society, involving persons who are trained in other disciplines or diverse disciplines and who have a broad rather than a specialized focus of interest. Activity is directed primarily at arousing concern about the problems rather than perfecting technical knowledge.

The *emerging phase* of professionalization is one in which limited funds are made available for exploring these problems, organizations are formed to conduct research and promote public support, schools or other educational programs are established to provide specialized training for persons who engage in such problem solving.

The *established phase* of professionalization is one in which the people involved begin to think in terms of careers rather than solving problems. It is characterized by a preoccupation with salaries, job classifications, and boundary definition. Specialization of knowledge within

1 Harold L. Wilensky and Charles N. Lebeaux, *Industrial Society and Social Welfare* (New York: Russell Sage Foundation, 1958), pp. 284f.

2 Martin Meyerson, "Five Functions for Planning," in *Urban Government, A Reader in Administration and Politics*, ed. Banfield., pp. 585f.

the field becomes more important than enlarging the scope of public concern. The established phase is characterized by imperialism rather than interdisciplinary collaboration.

Social-structural change as a professional technology   Now that we have described the nature of professionalism and the stages in its development, it is possible to discuss the relationship of social-structural change to professional practice.

On the first count, that of constituting a definitive area of technical competence, social-structural change qualifies as a type of professional practice. It has an integrating principle, namely the concept of social structures; and there is at least a rudimentary elaboration of knowledge about the nature of such structures and the effects of their change.

In fact social-structural change, as a theoretical framework for social planning, counteracts one of the principal criticisms levelled against attempts to define social planning in other than sectorial terms. We recall that the assumption underlying sectorial planning is that all human problems reduce eventually to the knowledge encompassed by one of the socially-oriented professions. According to this view, planning which cuts across professional domain boundaries involves an accumulation of areas of competence which is impossible to master and which lacks any integrating principle. In contrast, social-structural change constitutes a new way of cutting into social problems; it traverses rather than encompasses the areas of practice of the established professions.

However on the second count, that of exclusiveness, social-structural change cannot be considered an appropriate technological basis for defining professional practice. For example, policy making as a tool of intervention, is a method which the administrator or executive of any large organization has to utilize, regardless of his professional field of operation. Similarly, community organizing, while largely identified as a method of social work practice, is widely used as a professional technology by public health personnel in promoting better health standards and practices and by educators in extending the benefits of education beyond the confines of the school. Even land use controls which tend to be identified as a technology exclusive to city planning, are used by realtors and businessmen as a means of achieving their objectives.

In fact, social-structural change as a technology is antithetical to the notion of professionalism. In terms of the Meyerson analysis, it is problem-focused rather than domain-focused. It is eclectic in methodology since its uniqueness lies in its conceptualization of the object of change rather than the tools of change. It is more akin to the pre-professional phase of problem solving than to the established phase of professionalization.

The uniqueness of social-structural change as a method of social problem solving creates a dependence, not on some area of professional competence, but rather on certain positions within a decision-making structure. To accomplish social-structural change, the change agent must be in a position to influence a given system of social relationships through exercising control over some critical resources. These resources have to do with the use of land, the aggregation of populations, the administration of organizations, the expenditure of public monies, and the enactment and interpretation of law. Such positions could be filled by persons from almost any of the existing socially-oriented professions, such as social work, education, city planning, health, or law, providing that the individuals involved have an understanding of the nature of social change.

There are, moreover, certain types of structures in which this function would more likely occur. For example, social-structural change as a technology is more suited to public rather than to private decision-making structures, since most of the tools of intervention require acts of governmental or legally-constituted bodies. Nevertheless, even within the confines of a voluntary agency, for example a children's institution, social-structural change is possible with regard to the system of social relationships contained within that institution.

A second discriminating characteristic of such structures of decision making is that they constitute an interdisciplinary or nondisciplinary setting rather than one coincident with the domain of an established profession. The reason for this is self-evident. By definition, social-structural change is problem-centered rather than practice-centered. Within an established profession practice tends to be more concerned with the preservation and expansion of the profession's domain rather than with the solution of problems. Social-structural change is premised on the assumption that the solution to problems lies in rearranging the social environment rather than in the application of a professional service. The knowledge necessary to guide such change derives from a variety of disciplines, sociology, economics, political science; and the tools available to accomplish such change depend on the competencies of various professions, including social work, education, law, and city planning.

Consequently, positions compatible to the exercise of social-structural change are more likely in decision-making structures which are not clearly identified with one of the established social service professions. For example, the mayor's office, or budget bureaus of the federal or

state governments, are likely to be less concerned with domain preservation than actual operating departments such as welfare, health, education, or housing. Similarly, city planning departments, even though they
coincide with one of the socially-oriented professions, are divorced from
the responsibility for operating a direct-service program with its accompanying pressures for professionalization.

IMPLICATIONS FOR PROFESSIONAL EDUCATION

There remains the question, how does one train practitioners to
engage in social-structural change?

If social-structural change as a technology does not fall within the
domain of any one profession, and if it can be implemented through a
variety of tools in any system of social relationships, then it would be
natural to conclude that relevant training should be built into the educational program of every socially-oriented profession. Social-structural
change can be thought of as a new way for each profession to attack
the social problems with which it is confronted with the resources at
its disposal.

For example, within the profession of social work, administrators and
social welfare planners could be trained to see the problems of mental
health and child welfare in terms of the system of social relationships in
which patients and children live, be they treatment institutions, adoptive
families, or residential settings. The kind of analysis fostered by Rosow
is relevant. Synanon and Alcoholics Anonymous are obvious examples
of such an approach. Carpenter's analysis of status degradation has implications for the treatment of social deviants.

Social-structural change has obvious implications for the field of
education. The individual classroom becomes a social system in which
learning or the lack thereof is a problem state. Educators are beginning
to think about the composition of the classroom as well as the respective
roles and statuses of students vis-à-vis teachers in fostering learning.

In the field of city planning, the applications have already been
indicated. City planners in their proposals for land use and capital
expenditures have a direct impact on forming the systems of social
interaction in which people are involved.

A less clear case is the field of health. Here the distinction must be
made between health problems which have an exclusive physiological
origin and health problems in which social interaction may be a heavy
contributing factor. For example, alcoholism and mental illness are
known to have an etiology stemming from social relationships. In this
case, social-structural change may have an important bearing on treat-

ment itself. For other kinds of health problems social-structural change may only be relevant in terms of the organization of treatment facilities and their use by target populations. Herbert Gans has conveyed this impact of social systems in his study *The Urban Villagers*.[3]

However, social-structural change makes possible a new approach to training people for careers in social planning. Since the integrating principle in this view of planning is change in systems of social relationships rather than the tools specific to any one profession, it should be possible to develop training programs on an interdisciplinary basis. Such programs could bring together lawyers, social workers, public health officials, city planners, and educators around a common interest in structural change; one in which each could contribute knowledge about techniques accumulated within his own field which has relevance for structural change as a method of problem solving.

For example, housing policies and land use controls have been identified more traditionally with city planning. Community organization has been identified with the field of social work, and to some extent adult education and public health. Administrative regulation is characteristic of all professions. The formulation of legislation and the use of judicial processes has of course been the traditional domain of the legal profession. It is interesting to note that most of the socially-oriented professions are beginning to introduce law courses into their curricula. This tendency of social change to cut across the professions in terms of a skill base, makes interdisciplinary education not only possible but desirable.

An interdisciplinary training program in social planning could do much to overcome two existing barriers to effective problem solving on the part of the socially-oriented professions. One is the barrier to communication and collaboration; housing experts and community organizers, health officers and lawyers, educators and social workers often lack a common ground, a common frame of reference for reaching agreement on social policies for issues of mutual concern.

A second barrier to be overcome is the tendency of established professions to define social problems in terms of the tools or techniques over which they claim exclusive competence, such as counseling, education, or medical care. Social problems such as poverty, racism, and violence do not lend themselves to such narrow treatments. While social-structural change has its own defining limits, they are broader. As the basis of an interdisciplinary training program, such a framework could provide an atmosphere for all of the socially-oriented professions to be more eclectic in their approach to social problems.

3 Herbert J. Gans, *The Urban Villagers* (New York: The Free Press, 1962).

And lastly, on a more general level, the concept of social-structural change is relevant to the very real need to prepare people for citizenship in a dynamic society. The frequent reference in public discussions to the rapid pace of social change reflects the growing public awareness that social change is a fact of social life. If we are to live in a dynamic society, we must accept social change as a normal state of affairs, and learn how to recognize and be responsive to the need for it.

For two generations American culture has undergone profound changes as a result of mass education about the dynamics of individual growth and behavior, a legacy of the Freudian revolution. It is not so long ago that American mothers believed that thumb sucking would lead to mal-occlusions of the teeth.

In the 1960s the social ferment and conflict accompanying the self-conscious awareness of poverty, racism, and violence within American society, created the need for a mass education about the care and feeding of social systems.

An alternative to such an approach is threatened by the revolutionaries. Their thesis is that systems do not change in response to human need; that social change cannot originate from within. They believe that the present system must be destroyed in order to build anew. The alternative to such a dire remedy is an enlightened citizenship that can understand the need for social change, both in terms of making a better life for disadvantaged segments of society, as well as preserving a future for itself.

BIBLIOGRAPHY

BERUBE, MAURICE R. and MARILYN GITTELL, eds. *Confrontation at Ocean Hill-Brownsville.* New York: Frederick A. Praeger, Inc., 1969.

BLAU, PETER M. "Formal Organization: Dimensions of Analysis," *American Journal of Sociology, 63* (July 1957), 58–69.

BOGUE, DONALD. *Skid Row in American Cities.* Chicago: University of Chicago, Community and Family Study Center, 1963.

BRAGER, GEORGE A. and HARRY SPECHT, "Social Action by the Poor: Prospects, Problems, and Strategies," *Community Action Against Poverty.* Eds. George A. Brager and Francis P. Purcell. New Haven, Conn.: College and University Press, 1967.

CANCIAN, FRANCESCA. "Functional Analysis of Change," *Social Change.* Eds. Amitai Etzioni and Eva Etzioni. New York: Basic Books, Inc., Publishers, 1964.

CLOWARD, RICHARD A. and LLOYD E. OHLIN, *Delinquency and Opportunity.* New York: The Free Press, 1960.

COLEMAN, JAMES S. *Community Conflict.* New York: The Free Press, 1957.

COONS, JOHN E., WILLIAM H. CLUNE, III, and STEPHAN D. SUGARMAN. "Educational Opportunity: A Workable Constitutional Test for State Financial Structures," *California Law Review, 57* (April 1969), 305–421.

COSER, LEWIS A. *Continuities in the Study of Social Conflict.* New York: The Free Press, 1967.

COUNCIL ON SOCIAL WORK EDUCATION. *Community Organization Curriculum Development Project.* Waltham, Mass.: Florence Heller Graduate School for Advanced Studies in Social Welfare, Brandeis University, 1968.

DAVIDOFF, PAUL. "Advocacy and Pluralism in Planning," *Journal of the American Institute of Planners, 31* (November 1965), 331–38.

DAVIS, JAMES A. "A Formal Interpretation of the Theory of Relative Deprivation," *Sociometry, 22* (December 1959), 280–96.

DAVIS, JAMES A., JOE L. SPAETH, and CAROLINE HUSON. "A Technique for Analyzing the Effects of Group Composition," *American Sociological Review, 26* (April 1961), 215–26.

DEUTSCH, MORTON and MARY EVANS COLLINS. "Interracial Housing," *American Social Patterns.* Ed. William Peterson. Garden City, N. Y.: Doubleday & Company, Inc., 1965.

DUNHAM, H. WARREN. "Community Psychiatry: The Newest Therapeutic Bandwagon,'" *The Sociology of Mental Disorders.* Ed. S. Kirson Weinberg. Chicago: Aldine Publishing Co., 1967.

DURKHEIM, ÉMILE. *The Rules of Sociological Method, 8th ed.,* trans. Sara Solovay and John Mueller. New York: The Free Press, 1964.

DURKHEIM, ÉMILE. *Suicide.* Trans. John A. Spaulding and George Simpson. New York: The Free Press, 1951.

FLYNN, MICHAEL. "Community Control of the Public School—Practical Approach for Achieving Educational Opportunity: a Socio-legal Perspective." *Suffolk University Law Review, 3* (Spring 1969), 308–43.

FRIEDEN, BERNARD J. "The Changing Prospects for Social Planning," *Journal of the American Institute of Planners, 33* (September 1967), 311–23.

GANS, HERBERT J. *People and Plans.* New York: Basic Books, Inc., Publishers, 1968.

GANS, HERBERT J. *The Urban Villagers.* New York: The Free Press, 1962.

HAGGSTROM, WARREN C. "The Power of the Poor," *Mental Health of the Poor.* Eds. Frank Reissman, Jerome Cohen, and Arthur Pearl. New York: The Free Press, 1964.

HOVIS, BARRY D. "New York City School Decentralization," *Prospectus, 3* (December 1969), 228–37.

JACOBS, JANE. *The Death and Life of Great American Cities.* New York: Random House, Inc., 1961.

KAHN, ALFRED J. "From Delinquency Treatment to Community Development," *The Uses of Sociology.* Eds. Paul F. Lazersfeld, William H. Seawall, and Harold L. Wilensky. New York: Basic Books, Inc., Publishers, 1967.

KAHN, ALFRED J. "Social Science and the Conceptual Framework for Community Organization Research," *Social Science Theory and Social Work Research.* Ed. Leonard S. Kogan. New York: National Association of Social Workers, 1960.

KATZ, DANIEL and ROBERT L. KAHN. *The Social Psychology of Organizations.* New York: John Wiley & Sons, Inc., 1966.

KOZOL, JONATHAN. *Death at an Early Age.* Boston: Houghton Mifflin Company, 1967.

LEIGHTON, ALEXANDER H. *An Introduction to Social Psychiatry.* Springfield, Ill.: Charles C Thomas, 1960.

LEIGHTON, ALEXANDER H., JOHN A. CLAUSEN, and ROBERT N. WILSON. eds. *Explorations in Social Psychiatry.* New York: Basic Books, Inc., Publishers, 1957.

LINDBLOM, CHARLES E. *The Policy-Making Process.* Englewood Cliffs, N.J.: Prentice-Hall, Inc., 1968.

LINTON, RALPH. *The Study of Man.* New York: Appleton-Century-Crofts, 1936.

MERTON, ROBERT K. *Social Theory and Social Structure,* 1968 ed. New York: The Free Press, 1968.

MILLER, S. M. and FRANK RIESSMAN. *Social Class and Social Policy.* New York: Basic Books, Inc., Publishers, 1968.

MOBILIZATION FOR YOUTH, INC. *A Proposal for the Prevention and Control of Delinquency by Expanding Opportunities.* New York: Mobilization for Youth, Inc., 1961.

NATIONAL ASSOCIATION OF HOUSING and REDEVELOPMENT OFFICIALS, and NATIONAL SOCIAL WELFARE ASSEMBLY. *Working Together for Urban Renewal, A Guide on Why, When, and How Social Welfare Agencies and Urban Renewal Agencies Should Work Together.* Chicago: National Association of Housing and Redevelopment Officials, 1958.

NISBET, ROBERT A. *Émile Durkheim.* Englewood Cliffs, N. J.: Prentice-Hall, Inc., 1965.

NISBET, ROBERT A. *Social Change and History.* New York: Oxford University Press, 1969.

PARSONS, TALCOTT. *The Social System.* New York: The Free Press, 1951.

PARSONS, TALCOTT. *The Structure of Social Action.* New York: The Free Press, 1949.

PEARL, ARTHUR and FRANK RIESSMAN. *New Careers for the Poor.* New York: The Free Press, 1965.

PERLOFF, HARVEY S. "New Directions in Social Planning," *Journal of American Institute of Planners, 31* (November 1965), 297–304.

POPE, LISTON. *Millhands and Preachers.* New Haven, Conn.: Yale University Press, 1942.

RADER, R. M. "Demise of the Neighborhood School Plan," *Cornell Law Review, 55* (April 1970), 594–610.

RAMSÖY, ODD. *Social Groups as System and Subsystem.* New York: The Free Press, 1963.

ROSENBERG, MORRIS. *Society and the Adolescent Self-Image.* Princeton, N. J.: Princeton University Press, 1965.

ROSOW, IRVING. *Social Integration of the Aged.* New York: The Free Press, 1957.

ROSS, MURRAY C. *Community Organization Theory and Principles.* New York: Harper & Row, Publishers, 1955.

ROUSSELOT, PETER F. "Achieving Equal Educational Opportunity for Negroes in the Public Schools of the North and West: The Emerging Role for Private Constitutional Litigation," *The George Washington Law Review.* 35 (May 1967), 698–720.

SHAPIRO, JOAN H. "Single-Room Occupancy: Community of the Alone," *Social Work, 11* (October 1966) 24–34.

SIMMEL, GEORGE. *Conflict and the Web of Group Affiliations.* Trans. Kurt H. Wolff and Reinhard Bendix. New York: The Press, 1955.

STINCHCOMBE, ARTHUR L. *Constructing Social Theories.* New York: Harcourt Brace Jovanovich, Inc., 1968.

VALENTINE, CHARLES A. *Culture and Poverty.* Chicago: University of Chicago Press, 1968.

WALLACE, WALTER L. *Sociological Theory.* Chicago: Aldine Publishing Company, 1969.

WARREN, ROLAND L. *The Community in America.* Chicago: Rand McNally & Co., 1963.

WEBBER, MELVIN M. "Comprehensive Planning and Social Responsibility," *Urban Planning and Social Policy.* Ed. Bernard J. Frieden and Robert Morris. New York: Basic Books, Inc., Publishers, 1968.

WEINBERG, S. KIRSON. "Psychiatric Sociology: The Sociology of Mental Disorders," *The Sociology of Mental Disorders,* Ed. S. Kirson Weinberg. Chicago: Aldine Publishing Co., 1967.

WILNER, DANIEL M., ROSABELLE PRICE WALKLEY, and STUART W. COOK. *Human Relations in Interracial Housing.* Minneapolis: University of Minnesota Press, 1955.

WISEMAN, JACQUELINE P. *Stations of the Lost.* Englewood Cliffs, N. J.: Prentice-Hall, Inc., 1970.

WITMER, HELEN L. *Social Work, An Analysis of a Social Institution.* New York: Holt, Rinehart & Winston, Inc., 1942.

WORKS, ERNEST. "The Prejudice-interaction Hypothesis From the Point of View of the Negro Minority Group," *The American Journal of Sociology,* 67 (July 1961), 47–53.

INDEX

NOTES

NOTES